Mexican Immigrants

José Ruiz

Immigration to North America

Mexican Immigrants

José Ruiz

Senior Consulting Editor Stuart Anderson
former Associate Commissioner for Policy and Planning,
US. Citizenship and Immigration Services

Introduction by Marian L. Smith, Historian,
U.S. Citizenship and Immigration Services

Introduction by Peter A. Hammerschmidt,
former First Secretary, Permanent Mission of Canada to the United Nations

MASON CREST
PHILADELPHIA

Mason Crest
450 Parkway Drive, Suite D
Broomall, PA 19008
www.masoncrest.com

©2017 by Mason Crest, an imprint of National Highlights, Inc.

Printed and bound in the United States of America.

CPSIA Compliance Information: Batch #INA2016.
For further information, contact Mason Crest at 1-866-MCP-Book.

First printing
1 3 5 7 9 8 6 4 2

Library of Congress Cataloging-in-Publication Data

on file at the Library of Congress
ISBN: 978-1-4222-3688-8 (hc)
ISBN: 978-1-4222-8105-5 (ebook)

Immigration to North America series ISBN: 978-1-4222-3679-6

Table of Contents

KEY ICONS TO LOOK FOR:

Words to Understand: These words with their easy-to-understand definitions will increase the reader's understanding of the text, while building vocabulary skills.

Sidebars: This boxed material within the main text allows readers to build knowledge, gain insights, explore possibilities, and broaden their perspectives by weaving together additional information to provide realistic and holistic perspectives.

Research Projects: Readers are pointed toward areas of further inquiry connected to each chapter. Suggestions are provided for projects that encourage deeper research and analysis.

Text-Dependent Questions: These questions send the reader back to the text for more careful attention to the evidence presented there.

Series Glossary of Key Terms: This back-of-the book glossary contains terminology used throughout this series. Words found here increase the reader's ability to read and comprehend higher-level books and articles in this field.

The Changing Face of the United States

Marian L. Smith, Historian
U.S. Citizenship and Immigration Services

Americans commonly assume that immigration today is very different than immigration of the past. The immigrants themselves appear to be unlike immigrants of earlier eras. Their language, their dress, their food, and their ways seem strange. At times people fear too many of these new immigrants will destroy the America they know. But has anything really changed? Do new immigrants have any different effect on America than old immigrants a century ago? Is the American fear of too much immigration a new development? Do immigrants really change America more than America changes the immigrants? The very subject of immigration raises many questions.

In the United States, immigration is more than a chapter in a history book. It is a continuous thread that links the present moment to the first settlers on North American shores. From the first colonists' arrival until today, immigrants have been met by Americans who both welcomed and feared them. Immigrant contributions were always welcome—on the farm, in the fields, and in the factories. Welcoming the poor, the persecuted, and the "huddled masses" became an American principle. Beginning with the original Pilgrims' flight from religious persecution in the 1600s, through the Irish migration to escape starvation in the 1800s, to the relocation of Central Americans seeking refuge from civil wars in the 1980s and 1990s, the United States has considered itself a haven for the destitute and the oppressed.

But there was also concern that immigrants would not adopt American ways, habits, or language. Too many immigrants might overwhelm America. If so, the dream of the Founding Fathers for United States government and society would be destroyed. For this reason, throughout American history some have argued that limiting or ending immigration is our patriotic duty. Benjamin Franklin feared there were so many German immigrants in Pennsylvania the Colonial Legislature would begin speaking German. "Progressive" leaders of the early 1900s feared that immigrants who could not read and understand the English language were not only exploited by "big business," but also served as the foundation for "machine politics" that undermined the U.S. Constitution. This theme continues today, usually voiced by those who bear no malice toward immigrants but who want to preserve American ideals.

Have immigrants changed? In colonial days, when most colonists were of English descent, they considered Germans, Swiss, and French immigrants as different. They were not "one of us" because they spoke a different language. Generations later, Americans of German or French descent viewed Polish, Italian, and Russian immigrants as strange. They were not "like us" because they had a different religion, or because they did not come from a tradition of constitutional government. Recently, Americans of Polish or Italian descent have seen Nicaraguan, Pakistani, or Vietnamese immigrants as too different to be included. It has long been said of American immigration that the latest ones to arrive usually want to close the door behind them.

It is important to remember that fear of individual immigrant groups seldom lasted, and always lessened. Benjamin Franklin's anxiety over German immigrants disappeared after those immigrants' sons and daughters helped the nation gain independence in the Revolutionary War. The Irish of the mid-1800s were among the most hated immigrants, but today we all wear green on St. Patrick's Day. While a century ago it was feared that Italian and other Catholic immigrants would vote as directed by the Pope, today that controversy is only a vague memory. Unfortunately, some ethnic groups continue their efforts to earn acceptance. The African

Americans' struggle continues, and some Asian Americans, whose families have been in America for generations, are the victims of current anti-immigrant sentiment.

Time changes both immigrants and America. Each wave of new immigrants, with their strange language and habits, eventually grows old and passes away. Their American-born children speak English. The immigrants' grandchildren are completely American. The strange foods of their ancestors—spaghetti, baklava, hummus, or tofu—become common in any American restaurant or grocery store. Much of what the immigrants brought to these shores is lost, principally their language. And what is gained becomes as American as St. Patrick's Day, Hanukkah, or Cinco de Mayo, and we forget that it was once something foreign.

Recent immigrants are all around us. They come from every corner of the earth to join in the American Dream. They will continue to help make the American Dream a reality, just as all the immigrants who came before them have done.

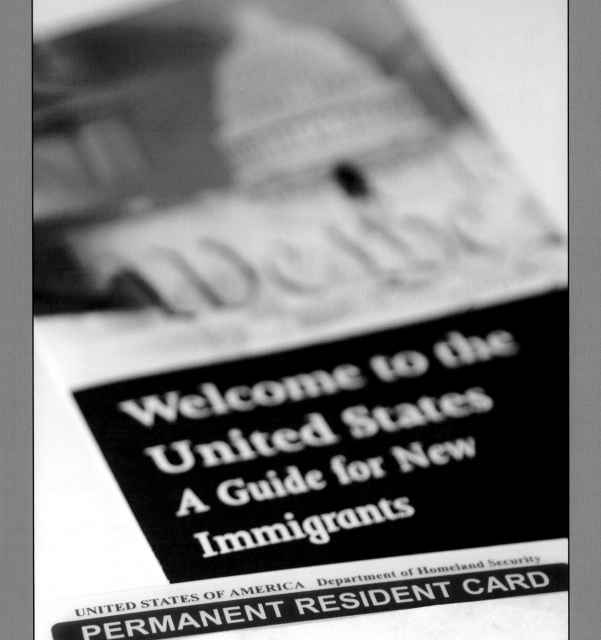

Welcome to the United States
A Guide for New Immigrants

UNITED STATES OF AMERICA   Department of Homeland Security
PERMANENT RESIDENT CARD

UNITED STATES OF AMER

We recommend you use this env
protect your new card.

The Changing Face of Canada

Peter A. Hammerschmidt
former First Secretary, Permanent Mission of Canada to the United Nations

Throughout Canada's history, immigration has shaped and defined the very character of Canadian society. The migration of peoples from every part of the world into Canada has profoundly changed the way we look, speak, eat, and live. Through close and distant relatives who left their lands in search of a better life, all Canadians have links to immigrant pasts. We are a nation built by and of immigrants.

Two parallel forces have shaped the history of Canadian immigration. The enormous diversity of Canada's immigrant population is the most obvious. In the beginning came the enterprising settlers of the "New World," the French and English colonists. Soon after came the Scottish, Irish, and Northern and Central European farmers of the 1700s and 1800s. As the country expanded westward during the mid-1800s, migrant workers began arriving from China, Japan, and other Asian countries. And the turbulent twentieth century brought an even greater variety of immigrants to Canada, from the Caribbean, Africa, India, and Southeast Asia.

So while English- and French-Canadians are the largest ethnic groups in the country today, neither group alone represents a majority of the population. A large and vibrant multicultural mix makes up the rest, particularly in Canada's major cities. Toronto, Vancouver, and Montreal alone are home to people from over 200 ethnic groups!

Less obvious but equally important in the evolution of Canadian immigration has been hope. The promise of a better life lured Europeans and

Americans seeking cheap (sometimes even free) farmland. Thousands of Scots and Irish arrived to escape grinding poverty and starvation. Others came for freedom, to escape religious and political persecution. Canada has long been a haven to the world's dispossessed and disenfranchised— Dutch and German farmers cast out for their religious beliefs, black slaves fleeing the United States, and political refugees of despotic regimes in Europe, Africa, Asia, and South America.

The two forces of diversity and hope, so central to Canada's past, also shaped the modern era of Canadian immigration. Following the Second World War, Canada drew heavily on these influences to forge trailblazing immigration initiatives.

The catalyst for change was the adoption of the Canadian Bill of Rights in 1960. Recognizing its growing diversity and Canadians' changing attitudes towards racism, the government passed a federal statute barring discrimination on the grounds of race, national origin, color, religion, or sex. Effectively rejecting the discriminatory elements in Canadian immigration policy, the Bill of Rights forced the introduction of a new policy in 1962. The focus of immigration abruptly switched from national origin to the individual's potential contribution to Canadian society. The door to Canada was now open to every corner of the world.

Welcoming those seeking new hopes in a new land has also been a feature of Canadian immigration in the modern era. The focus on economic immigration has increased along with Canada's steadily growing economy, but political immigration has also been encouraged. Since 1945, Canada has admitted tens of thousands of displaced persons, including Jewish Holocaust survivors, victims of Soviet crackdowns in Hungary and Czechoslovakia, and refugees from political upheaval in Uganda, Chile, and Vietnam.

Prior to 1978, however, these political refugees were admitted as an exception to normal immigration procedures. That year, Canada revamped its refugee policy with a new Immigration Act that explicitly affirmed Canada's commitment to the resettlement of refugees from oppression. Today, the admission of refugees remains a central part of

Canadian immigration law and regulations.

Amendments to economic and political immigration policy have continued, refining further the bold steps taken during the modern era. Together, these initiatives have turned Canada into one of the world's few truly multicultural states.

Unlike the process of assimilation into a "melting pot" of cultures, immigrants to Canada are more likely to retain their cultural identity, beliefs, and practices. This is the source of some of Canada's greatest strengths as a society. And as a truly multicultural nation, diversity is not seen as a threat to Canadian identity. Quite the contrary—diversity is Canadian identity.

1 MEXICAN AMERICANS

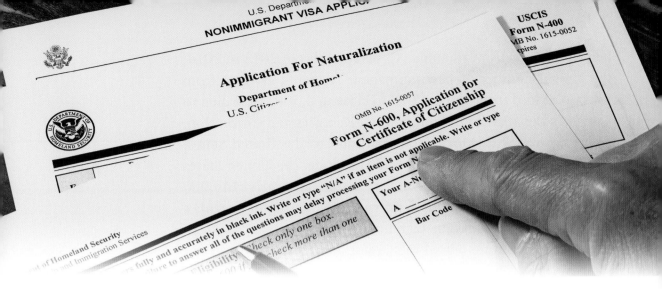

About 34 million people living in the United States today claim Mexican heritage. Some of them can trace their ancestors to the early settlers of the present-day U.S. Southwest, which was part of the Spanish colony of Nueva España (New Spain). Others came later, in waves of migration that occurred throughout the 20th century. Still others arrived a decade or two ago, while some entered the country even more recently.

Most northward migration from Mexico has ended within the boundaries of the United States. As of 1950, only a few Mexicans had chosen to live as far north as Canada, and they were mostly the Mexican-born children of Canadian Mennonites who had migrated to northern Mexico during the early 20th century. However, beginning in the 1970s, growing numbers of Mexicans made Canada their home.

According to Canada's 2011 census, nearly 69,700 people of Mexican descent had settled in the country—an increase of more than 92 percent from 2001. Almost 4 in 10 of these immigrants resided in the province of Ontario, with a large proportion of that group clustered in the Toronto metropolitan area. Quebec was the province with the next highest proportion of Canada's immigrants from Mexico (22 percent), followed by Alberta (15

◀ A group of men approach the U.S. border at Agua Prieta, Mexico. By 2015, over 11 million Mexican-born people were living in the United States—more than one-quarter of the total foreign-born population. The Mexican population in Canada has been expanding in recent decades, though it is still much lower than in the United States.

percent) and British Columbia (13 percent). From 2012 to 2014, the annual number of new permanent residents arriving from Mexico ranged from about 4,000 to close to 4,500, according to Canada's Department of Immigration, Refugees and Citizenship.

Compared with Mexican immigration to the United States, these numbers are quite small. In 2011 alone, the United States granted lawful permanent resident status to nearly 143,000 Mexican immigrants—more than twice the number of Canada's entire Mexican immigrant community for that year. Mexican Americans constitute one of the largest and most rapidly growing minority groups in the United States.

Geography and People

Directly south of the United States lies Mexico. The country, a federal republic, is made up of 31 states. At about 761,600 square miles (1,972,535 square kilometers), Mexico is approximately one-fifth the size of the United States in total area. The two countries share a border stretching 1,989 miles (3,200 km). More than 60 percent of that border, in the east, runs along a river—the Rio Grande. In the west, the border crosses through desert land before reaching the Pacific coast south of San Diego, California.

Mexico's land consists mostly of deserts, rugged mountains, high plateaus, and jungles. Only an estimated 10 percent of the land is good for farming.

 Words to Understand in This Chapter

entrepreneur—a person who organizes, operates, and assumes the financial risks of a business.

Hispanic—a person of Spanish or Latino descent.

mestizo—a person of mixed American Indian and Spanish ancestry.

La raza—"the race"; refers specifically to the people of Mexico.

recession—a temporary economic slump or decline.

Tejano—a Mexican American native to Texas.

In 2015 Mexico's population was estimated at nearly 122 million.

More than 60 percent of Mexico's people are mestizo—that is, of mixed Indian and Spanish ancestry. Mexico's indigenous peoples were conquered by Spain in the 16th century, and Spain ruled Mexico for almost 300 years. During that time Spanish settlers brought their language, religious faith, and traditions, which became incorporated into the mestizo culture.

About 15 to 30 percent of Mexicans are of American Indian ancestry, and a much smaller number are of European or African descent. Although the Mexican people may be diverse in appearance and culture, most are united by the Spanish language, the Catholic faith, and a strong sense of family and community.

Part of the Hispanic Culture

Since the 1960s, the U.S. Census Bureau (the government agency that records how many people live in the United States) has grouped all Spanish-speaking people together as Hispanic or Latino. This category includes people from Mexico, as well as from Puerto Rico, Cuba, the Dominican Republic, and other countries of Central and South America. For the most part, the terms Hispanic and Latino aren't used in Spanish-speaking countries.

Until recently Hispanics were the second-largest minority group in the United States, smaller only than the African-American population. But in mid-2001, according to the Census Bureau, Hispanics became the largest minority group. The number of Hispanics living in the United States grew from 22.4 million (9 percent of the population) in 1990 to 35.3 million (12 percent) in 2000. By 2013, the Census Bureau reported, the number of Hispanics living in the United States totaled 54 million—17 percent of the total U.S. population. More than half of this group has its roots in Mexico.

Because the terms Hispanic and Latino refer to people from so many different countries, races, and cultures, some Mexican Americans prefer to refer to themselves by other names that clearly define who they are. For example, Mexican Americans from Texas are Tejanos; in California they are Californios. During the 1950s and 1960s, many young Mexican Americans preferred the term Chicano, a shortened version of Mexicano, although their elders tended to disapprove of the word, which was previously used as an ethnic slur. But for younger generations, Chicano became a source of ethnic pride that acknowledged their connection to Mexico.

Mexican Americans may also belong to other racial groups (Caucasians, American Indians, Africans, or a mixture). However, they proudly consider themselves members of La raza, the same cultural and ethnic group whose heart lies in Mexico.

The Mexican and Mexican American Population

Demographers (people who study human population statistics) have developed different ways to count immigrants. For exam-

A Mexican family runs across the border between Tijuana, Mexico, and San Diego, California. Researchers estimated in 2014 that about 5.6 million Mexicans living in the United States did not have lawful immigration status.

ple, researchers trying to describe the Mexican population in the United States may look at the number of Mexican-born people residing in the country, the number of Mexicans who legally immigrate to the United States in a particular year, or the number of people living in the country who report Mexican heritage.

Mexican-born residents are first-generation immigrants, those who left the country of their birth to move to a new land. Census statistics of the foreign-born population indicate a strong, steady increase in the number of Mexican-born immigrants living in the United States. The total was about 576,000 in 1960; almost 760,000 in 1970; over 2 million in 1980; over 4 million in 1990; about 8 million in 2000; and 11.7 million in 2010, when the Census Bureau found that Mexicans accounted for more than 29 percent of the entire foreign-born population of the United States.

For decades, Mexicans have formed the largest group of legal immigrants (people lawfully admitted for permanent residence) to the United States. In 1960 about 32,000 Mexicans legally immigrated to the United States. In 1970 that number was nearly 65,000. It surpassed 100,000 in 1980 and approached 174,000 in 2000. Throughout the 1990s and into 2000 Mexicans accounted for approximately 20 percent of all legal immigrants. The numbers have declined somewhat in recent years. Still, the 134,000-plus Mexicans granted permanent resident status in 2013 constituted 13.5 percent of the total number of legal immigrants to the United States.

Mexicans have also accounted for a large percentage of undocumented immigrants entering the United States. (These are immigrants without legal paperwork, also referred to as "illegal immigrants.") Exact numbers are impossible to determine, but official estimates indicate that illegal Mexican migration rose steadily from 1960 to 1980 before exploding thereafter, with approximately 300,000 new arrivals each year through the end of the century.

According to the Pew Research Center, the total number of Mexicans living in the United States without proper authorization peaked in 2007, at about 6.9 million. By 2014 the number had fallen to an estimated 5.6 million. This decline, Pew researchers explained, occurred because more undocumented Mexicans were returning to their home country than were arriving in the United States. And that mostly reflected the weak state of the U.S. economy, which suffered a severe recession from late 2007 to mid-2009, with uneven job growth thereafter.

In 2012, according to the Census Bureau, approximately 33.7 million people—more than one-tenth of the total U.S. population—claimed Mexican ancestry. That number includes U.S. citizens whose families have lived in the country for generations, as well as recent immigrants.

Mexican American Culture

Mexican Americans have contributed a great deal to American culture. During the 1960s the Chicano movement united a large number of Mexican Americans seeking to obtain equal rights in politics, education, and the workplace through labor strikes and peaceful protest. During this time activist César Chávez organized farmworkers, while students protested poor conditions in inner-city schools and U.S. involvement in the Vietnam War. The Chicano movement represented more than a group's protests against discrimination and inequality; it also symbolized a new pride in Mexican identity.

That pride soon translated into the political action of the Chicano movement, as Mexican Americans organized voter registration drives and supported Hispanic candidates. Many Mexican Americans entered politics during this time. They ran for school boards, city councils, county councils, and state and federal legislatures. In 1974 two Mexican Americans were elected state governors: Jerry Apodaca in New Mexico and Raul Castro in Arizona. By 1980, six Hispanic Americans were serving in the U.S. Congress. By 2015, that number had increased to 32.

In 1976 U.S. representatives Henry B. González of Texas and Edward R. Roybal of California founded the Hispanic

Representative Henry B. González of Texas was a leading advocate for Latino causes. In 1976 he co-founded the Hispanic Congressional Caucus, an organization working to ensure that legislators debated the issues pertaining to Mexican Americans and other Latinos.

Congressional Caucus to ensure that the Latino voice was heard in the legislative debate. In 1981 Henry G. Cisneros became the first Mexican American elected mayor of a major U.S. city, San Antonio; he later served as secretary of the Department of Housing and Urban Development (HUD) under President Bill Clinton. Through the years other Mexican Americans have served in cabinet positions for various presidents: Katherine Ortega became treasurer of the United States under President Ronald Reagan; Manuel Lujan Jr. was secretary of the Department of the Interior under President George H. W. Bush; former Denver mayor Federico Peña headed the Department of Transportation under Clinton; President George W. Bush tapped Alberto Gonzales to be attorney general; and President Barack Obama appointed Julián Castro as HUD secretary.

Some believe that the Chicano movement also helped encourage Mexican American writing. One representative work from early in the movement is Rodolfo "Corky" Gonzales's epic poem, *I Am Joaquin* (1967). Other distinguished writers of essays, fiction, and poetry include Rudolfo A. Anaya, Sandra Cisneros, Ana Castillo, Richard Rodriguez, and Francisco Jiménez. Countless more have contributed to the growing field of Chicano literature, which is studied in universities across the United States.

During the 1990s, more doors opened to Hispanics, allowing Mexican and Mexican- American artists to make inroads in the entertainment industry. Latin-flavored singles and albums climbed the charts during the 1990s, with major contributions from Mexican-born guitarist Carlos Santana, Tejano pop star Selena, and the Los

Born in Mexico, Salma Hayek is widely recognized for her portrayals of Mexican and Mexican American characters. Her title performance in *Frida*, a biopic about the revolutionary Mexican painter Frida Kahlo, earned her an Oscar nomination in 2003.

Angeles–based rock group Los Lobos. Performing as Los Lonely Boys, brothers Henry, Jojo, and Ringo Garza scored a huge success in 2004 with their debut album.

The beginning of the 21st century saw more Mexican Americans portrayed on network television and in movies. Actors of Mexican ancestry—including Edward James Olmos, Eva Longoria, and Salma Hayek—landed leading roles. Mexican American comedians George Lopez and Gabriel Iglesias kept audiences laughing with their standup routines.

The roster of Mexican American sports stars is extensive. It includes golf legends Lee Trevino and Nancy Lopez; pro football quarterback Tony Romo and Hall of Fame lineman Anthony Muñoz; a slew of baseball players, such as Jake Arrieta, Andre Ethier, Nomar Garciaparra, and Evan Longoria; boxer Oscar de La Hoya, a two-time Olympic gold medalist and professional champion in six weight divisions; National Hockey League center Scott Gomez; and many more.

The Mexican influence has also reached into the kitchens and dining rooms of Americans. Chili, tacos, burritos, nachos, and enchiladas have become commonplace snacks and meals from coast to coast. Today, American consumers buy more salsa than catsup, and sales of tortillas outstrip those of hot dog or hamburger rolls.

Contributions to the U.S. Economy

One of the biggest impacts that Mexican immigrants have had on the United States is cumulative—years and years of hard work in jobs often shunned by others. These jobs, many in the fields of agriculture and industry, can be low-paying and low-prestige. Mexican immigrant workers have picked lettuce in California, apples in Washington, and oranges in Florida. They have harvested mushrooms in Pennsylvania, tobacco in North Carolina, and cotton in Texas; cleaned fish in Alaska; sewn garments in New York City and Los Angeles; and worked in the slaughterhouses of Iowa and Kansas.

In 2012, according to the U.S. Department of Agriculture, 68

César Chávez
Fighting for the Rights of Migrant Farmworkers

For decades Mexican migrant workers endured difficult living and working conditions. Housed in shacks without running water or electricity, farmworkers toiled 7 days a week for 15 cents an hour.

During the 1960s, a former migrant worker named César Chávez sought to bring about change through labor union action. In 1962 Chávez and activist Delores Huerta founded the National Farmworkers Association (NFWA) in Delano, California. Three years later Chávez organized a strike against grape growers in Delano County. This protest eventually evolved into a nationwide grape boycott that lasted five years. Its resolution brought about improved housing, health benefits, and wages for workers. In 1966, the NFWA merged with another union, creating the United Farmworkers (UFW), AFL-CIO.

Chávez led other labor actions against California lettuce growers, as well as organizing additional grape boycotts. He served as head of the UFW until his death in April 1993. A steadfast believer in the effectiveness of nonviolent protest, Chávez was posthumously honored with the Presidential Medal of Freedom, the highest civilian honor in the United States, in 1994.

percent of all hired crop farmworkers in the United States were born in Mexico. Conditions for these laborers—particularly for the approximately one-half not legally authorized to work in the United States—can be very difficult.

In addition to agriculture, Mexican immigrants have made up a substantial share of the workforces of several major U.S. industries. These include construction, meatpacking, and the hotel and restaurant industries.

Of course, Mexican immigrants aren't only laborers and low-wage workers. For many, the American dream includes starting their own business. In fact, according to the Partnership for a New American Economy—an organization that advocates for immigration reform—Mexican immigrants exceed native-born Americans in their propensity to become entrepreneurs. Between 1990 and 2012, according to a report released in 2015 by the Partnership for a New American Economy, "the number of self-employed Mexican immigrants grew by a factor of 5.4, reaching

765,000. Entrepreneurship became so established among Mexican immigrants that by 2012 more than one in 10 such immigrants was an entrepreneur." As the report noted, these entrepreneurs—many of whom are small-business owners specializing in providing products and services geared toward the Latino population—"helped power the economy during the recent recession."

 Text-Dependent Questions

1. Which Canadian province has the largest number of residents of Mexican descent?

2. Which river forms the eastern part of the U.S.-Mexico border?

3. In the 1960s, a movement aimed at empowering Mexican Americans began. By what name was that movement known?

 Research Project

Using a library or the Internet, investigate one of Mexico's 31 states or the Federal District (Mexico City). In a box, present the following basic information: Total area; Highest point; Lowest point; Population; Capital city; Other major cities. Then write a three or four paragraphs on any aspects of the state or Federal District that you found especially interesting.

2 THE STRUGGLE TO PROVIDE A LIVING

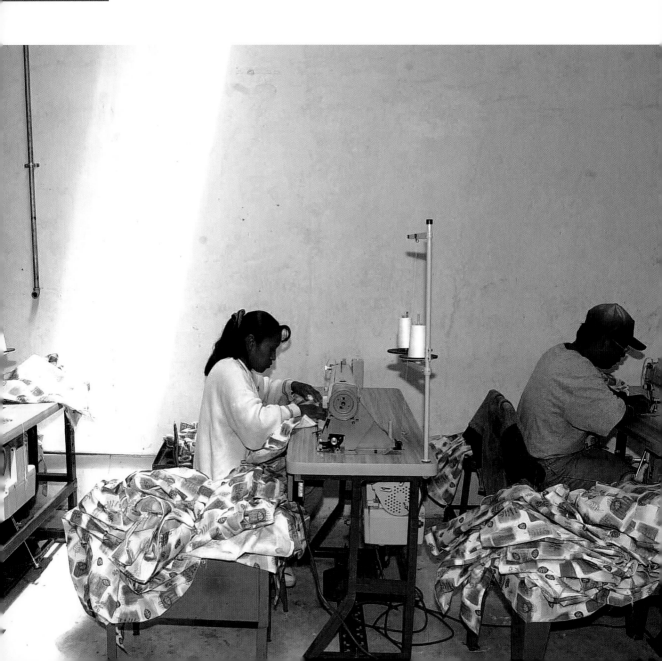

For most people, the decision to leave the land of their birth does not come easily. Sometimes extreme events such as political upheaval or national disasters leave victims no choice but to migrate. In a few instances during the past century, Mexican migrations have resulted because of war and catastrophe. In 1910 a bloody revolution drove millions of Mexican refugees to safety in the north. In 1985 thousands left Mexico City in search of new homes and lives when a major earthquake killed 10,000 people and destroyed entire blocks of buildings. In 2006 the Mexican government launched a crackdown on powerful drug cartels that traffic illegal drugs to the United States. Over the following decade, tens of thousands of ordinary Mexicans lost their lives as the cartels battled Mexican troops—and as the cartels fought one another to expand their share of the lucrative drug trade. Some areas of Mexico became so dangerous that many residents sought to immigrate to the United States.

Over the years, however, less dramatic factors have driven most migration from Mexico. Millions of Mexicans have been drawn to the United States by the prospect of greater economic opportunity.

◀ Mexican workers sew women's garments in one of the many maquiladoras found just south of the U.S.–Mexico border. These U.S.–owned factories employ a great segment of the Mexican workforce, though laborers are attracted to the less-grueling, higher-paying jobs that are often found north of the border.

Economic Migration

The border between Mexico and the United States stretches east to west, from near Brownsville, Texas (on the Gulf coast), to Tijuana, Mexico (at the beaches of the Pacific Ocean). This line separates two worlds—one where extreme poverty is not uncommon and the other where wealth abounds.

Mexico is a developing country. In recent decades it has made significant strides in expanding its economy and reducing poverty among its people. Nevertheless, Mexico's economic growth has been highly uneven. The Mexican economy continues to have trouble creating a sufficient number of jobs for the country's growing population, and about half of all Mexicans live below the official poverty line.

In 2014, according to a method used by the World Bank to compare economic conditions across countries, annual per capita (average) income in Mexico was estimated at $9,860. To the north, meanwhile, 2014 per capita income in the United States stood at $55,200, and the figure for Canada was $51,690.

The large income gap between Mexico and its North American neighbors has existed for more than a century. Given that fact, along with a dearth of job opportunities in many parts of Mexico, particularly rural areas, it's not surprising that millions of Mexicans have traveled north. They've dreamed of a better life for themselves and their families.

 Words to Understand in This Chapter

cartel—a combination of independent commercial enterprises designed to limit competition.

maquiladora—an assembly plant in Mexico; also called a "maquila."

per capita—by or for each person; per unit of population.

staple—a food that is eaten routinely and that forms a dominant portion of a group's diet.

tariff—a tax paid on goods coming into or leaving a country.

A busy intersection in Mexico City, the capital of Mexico. During the country's recession in the 1980s, many city workers, along with rural laborers, lost their jobs and migrated to the United States in search of work.

Mexico's Efforts to Create Jobs

During the 1940s, the Mexican government first began taking steps to reduce the economy's dependence on agriculture and mining. By industrializing the country, the government hoped to create more jobs for the unemployed (out of work) and under-employed (people working at a part-time job when they want full-time employment, or people working at a lower-skill job than they're trained or educated for).

Among the government's initiatives was the creation in 1965 of industrial zones along the border with the United States. In these areas, foreign companies could establish assembly plants, called maquiladoras, that had special privileges. Factory owners would pay minimal taxes and utility costs. The government would provide subsidies and drop import tariffs on materials coming to the plants. The finished manufactured products would then be shipped back north. By promoting intense industrial growth, Mexican officials hoped the country could benefit from foreign investment while reducing unemployment.

Lured by an abundant labor supply of ready workers, American companies, as well as firms from other countries, built maquiladoras throughout these industrial zones. In 1970 more than 200 such factories had been built, with about 19,000 employees in all. By the end of 1990 there were almost 2,000 factories, employing 500,000. And by the late 1990s more than 2,500 maquiladoras provided jobs for over one million workers living along the border.

Most maquiladora work was hard, usually consisting of long hours of repetitive tasks. The assembly plants tended to hire young women, who accepted lower pay than men. Wages ranged from $3 to $9 a day, which was much lower than salaries for comparable work in the United States. While northern Mexico was offering much-needed job opportunities, just over the border workers could find higher-paying jobs.

Meanwhile, the maquiladora program created boomtowns, as Mexicans from central and southern Mexico flocked to the northern regions in search of jobs.

The growth in Mexico's border towns brought a new challenge: how to provide for the overwhelming number of residents. Many people lived in shantytowns without electricity or water. Raw sewage and waste from both residential and industrial areas flowed into nearby rivers, while industrial toxins were disposed of along roadsides. The maquiladora industry created environmental problems that the Mexican government did not have the will or the resources to prevent.

A Faltering Economy

During the 1970s, Mexico entered a brief period of prosperity, resulting in part from the discovery of major petroleum deposits on the coast of the Gulf of Mexico. Soon the country became a major exporter to the United States. Anticipating large revenues because of the high price of oil, the Mexican government borrowed heavily from banks in the United States and Europe to cover costs for major construction projects. Then in the early

The First Mexican Americans

In 1848 the Mexican government signed the Treaty of Guadalupe Hidalgo, which outlined terms ending the Mexican War (1846–48). The pact gave away a large section of territory claimed by Mexico (present-day Texas, California, Nevada, and Utah, as well as parts of Colorado, New Mexico, and Wyoming). Later, the United States paid Mexico $15 million for the land, and in 1853, another $10 million (the Gadsden Purchase) for southern Arizona and New Mexico.

These transactions affected approximately 80,000 Mexican settlers and their descendants living in what had been northern Mexico but was now the U.S. Southwest. As a popular expression of Tejanos goes, "We never crossed a border. The border crossed us."

According to the terms of the Treaty of Guadalupe Hidalgo, these first Mexican Americans were granted U.S. citizenship and legal protection. However, the Mexican and American cultures did not mesh easily. Within just a few years the English-language U.S. courts and some disreputable American speculators had cheated Mexican landowners out of large tracts of property. By the late 1800s the majority of these first Mexican Americans were landless second-class citizens living in poverty and working at low-wage jobs.

1980s, the price of oil fell, and Mexico found itself with a large foreign debt it could not repay.

The resulting economic recession cost many Mexican workers their jobs. Many workers who were better educated and lived in cities joined the ranks of rural Mexicans migrating north in search of jobs during the 1980s. Urban workers, however, were seeking non-agricultural jobs.

Additional foreign investment and rescheduling of payment dates for loans helped Mexico's economy improve during the late 1980s and early 1990s. Other economic reforms made under President Carlos Salinas de Gortari (1988–94) and President Ernesto Zedillo (1994–2000) helped as well. Salinas and the ruling party, the Partido Revolucionario Institucional (PRI), worked to improve the economy by dropping tariffs that had protected Mexican industries but had also made them less efficient. Zedillo privatized many state-owned industries, meaning that banks, utilities, and airlines that had been run by the Mexican government were sold to private investors. Enrique Peña Nieto, who became president in 2012, pursued further eco-

Mexican president Carlos Salinas de Gortari, who led the country between 1988 and 1994, signed the landmark North American Free Trade Agreement (NAFTA) in 1991. The agreement, which lowered the prices of imports to Mexico, also sought to stem the tide of undocumented immigrants entering the U.S.

nomic reforms. He opened up Mexico's oil and gas fields to foreign investment, effectively ending a 75-year monopoly enjoyed by the state-owned Petróleos Mexicanos, or Pemex. At the same time, Peña Nieto championed reforms to the tax code to make Mexico less reliant on oil revenue.

Economists have generally approved of Mexico's economic reforms. Still, many scholars acknowledge that Mexico won't enjoy the full fruits of those reforms until significant changes are made to the country's political culture. Simply put, Mexico's government has a long-standing and well-earned reputation for corruption—and that hinders economic development.

North American Free Trade Agreement

During the 1990s, as Mexico pursued internal economic reforms, it also concluded a new trade agreement with the

United States and Canada. The North American Free Trade Agreement (NAFTA) aimed to facilitate the movement of goods, services, and money across borders by gradually eliminating tariffs and other trade barriers. On December 17, 1992, President George H. W. Bush of the United States, Prime Minister Brian Mulroney of Canada, and President Carlos Salinas de Gortari signed NAFTA. The accord went into effect in January 1994.

Supporters said that by increasing overall trade, NAFTA would create additional wealth in all three countries that were party to the agreement. In Mexico specifically, NAFTA was expected to boost U.S. and Canadian investment and to spur manufacturing growth. American and Canadian consumers would stand to benefit by being able to buy lower-cost products made in Mexico, and U.S. and Canadian companies would be able to sell additional goods and services to Mexicans.

Despite its touted benefits, NAFTA was controversial in the

Union workers in the United States protest against the passage of the North American Free Trade Agreement in 1992. American workers feared the loss of manufacturing jobs to Mexico.

United States. Many Americans feared the agreement would encourage U.S. manufacturers to move their production facilities south of the border, where labor costs were considerably cheaper. However, NAFTA's supporters insisted that job losses would be offset by the creation of new jobs. This, they argued, would come about because a growing Mexican middle class would purchase more American goods and services. Further, proponents of NAFTA suggested, increased prosperity in Mexico would lead to a smaller flow of undocumented immigrants seeking economic opportunity in the United States.

Two decades after NAFTA's implementation, its consequences remain controversial. It's safe to say, though, that NAFTA led to job losses in some U.S. industries, and to job gains in others. Economists disagree on the net effect.

For its part, Mexico saw an increase in manufacturing employment. On the other hand, Mexico's small farmers—the backbone of the country's agricultural sector—were devastated by the influx of cheap American corn and other staples. From 1994 to 2014, more than 2 million Mexican farmers who could no longer make a living were forced to abandon their land. Entire rural communities disappeared. Many of the displaced farmers and farmworkers headed north to the United States. Whatever other effects NAFTA may have had, most experts concede that it made the problem of undocumented immigration worse rather than better.

Social Unrest and Economic Anxiety

It didn't take long for worries about NAFTA, combined with discontent over poverty and the unfair practices of large farmers and ranchers, to spark major unrest in Mexico. In 1994 an armed uprising erupted in the southernmost state of Chiapas, home to many impoverished Indians. A group calling itself the Ejército Zapatista de Liberación Nacional (Zapatista Army of National Liberation) took over the state capital of San Cristóbal de Las Casas, demanding better social and economic opportunities. Believing that NAFTA would prevent the small farmers of

Members of the Ejército Zapatista de Liberación Nacional (EZLN), a rebel group, gather before a meeting. The Zapatistas, who united to fight the unjust practices of large farm owners, briefly took over the state capital of San Cristobal de Las Casas in 1994 before government forces crushed the rebellion.

Chiapas from getting a fair price for their crops and leave them open to economic exploitation, the Zapatistas also called for the "revision of the North American Free Trade Agreement signed with Canada and the United States, since [in] its present form it does not take into account the Indigenous population, and it sentences them to death because it does not include any labor qualifications whatsoever."

Although quickly routed by government troops, the Zapatistas continued to rebel against the Mexican government. Attempts to broker a peace agreement foundered, and protests and sporadic violence in Chiapas continued through 2014.

In 1994, as the Zapatista uprising was heating up, the Mexican government was forced to devalue the peso, the Mexican monetary unit, to reflect its true value against the American dollar. The value of the peso fell so low that foreign investors pulled their money out of Mexico. The nation suffered its worst economic recession in 50 years as inflation rates soared as much as 200 percent. From 1994 to 1995 the country's gross domestic product, or GDP (the value of all the goods and services produced annually in a nation) declined by 6.2 percent. A 1996 study by the prestigious Colegio de México found that 80 percent of the population lived in poverty.

Mexico's economy, which began to recover after the country received emergency loans from the U.S. government and the World Bank, expanded at a healthy rate during the last years of the 1990s and into 2000. But Mexico suffered a modest recession in 2001. A major recession rocked the country in 2008–2009, roughly coinciding with the so-called Great

An aerial view of Guanajuato City, the capital of Guanajuato. Along with two other western states, Jalisco and Michoacán, Guanajuato has consistently been a source of Mexican immigration to the United States.

President Vicente Fox of Mexico, who began his term in December 2000, speaks before the U.S. Congress. Among the major issues during Fox's initial years in office were immigration reform and the creation of economic incentives for Mexican workers to remain in the country.

Recession in the United States. Even though Mexico's unemployment and poverty rates spiked, economic conditions in the United States were also dismal, so undocumented immigration didn't increase dramatically. In fact, in the wake of the Great Recession there was a net outflow of unauthorized Mexican immigrants—fewer crossed into the United States than returned home to Mexico from the United States.

Political Change

A major political shift in Mexico took place in 2000. For the first time in 71 years, the ruling party—the PRI, or Partido Revolucionario Institucional (Institutional Revolutionary

Party)—lost the presidency. Mexican voters elected Vicente Fox of the Partido Acción Nacional (National Action Party). In the view of many political analysts and ordinary Mexicans alike, the PRI had become irredeemably corrupt after holding a virtual monopoly on the reins of government for seven decades. Over the years, a seemingly endless stream of PRI officials—from presidents and state governors to mayors and lesser bureaucrats—had enriched themselves at the public expense. The ruling party's lax attitude regarding corruption was perhaps best summed up by a PRI official named Carlos Hank González. "A politician who is poor," Hank said, "is a poor politician."

Mexicans hoped that the Partido Acción Nacional (PAN) and President Fox would bring a new emphasis on integrity to the government. During his six years as president, Fox did maintain an image of honesty. However, shortly after he left office, allegations of corruption surfaced—among them that Fox and his wife had renovated their ranch with public funds.

As president, Fox was a vocal advocate for undocumented Mexican immigrants in the United States. They took hard, low-paying jobs that American citizens were unwilling to do, Fox said. The Mexican president urged his U.S. counterpart, President George W. Bush, to pursue comprehensive immigration reform. Among other measures, Fox wanted the United States to institute a guest worker program for Mexicans. This, he believed, would allow the United States to fill its labor needs while protecting Mexicans from the kind of exploitation that undocumented workers frequently face. "The best thing that can happen to both our countries," Fox said, "is to have an orderly flow, a controlled flow, of migration to the United States."

By all accounts, Bush was receptive to Fox's ideas. But when terrorists attacked the United States on September 11, 2001, immigration reform took a backseat to national security issues.

By 2006, however, Bush had once again turned his attention to immigration reform. He urged Congress to pass legislation that would create a guest worker program and also enable illegal immigrants who were already in the United States to eventu-

Hundreds of thousands of immigrants, many of them Mexicans, participate in a Los Angeles march protesting against an immigration reform measure proposed by the U.S. Congress, May 2006.

ally obtain American citizenship. Congress considered several bills, but ultimately none passed.

Dreams of a Better Life

There is no "typical" Mexican immigrant. A 2001 study of Mexican immigration to the United States published in the *Latin American Research Review* found that most Mexican migrants were working-age males between the ages of 18 and 35. According to the study's authors—Jorge Durand, Douglas S. Massey, and René M. Zenteno—the proportion of Mexican men and women immigrating to the United States from 1970 through 1994 remained consistent, at 75 percent male and 25 percent female. But more recent data point to an increased percentage of female migrants. In 2008, according to the U.S. Census Bureau, more than three-quarters of Mexican immigrants were of working age, but males outnumbered females by just 55.8 percent to 44.2 percent.

Additionally, in recent years more Mexican children—many of them unaccompanied by adults—have been trying to enter the United States without proper documents. From October 2012 to May 2014, U.S. Border Patrol agents apprehended nearly 29,000 unaccompanied Mexican minors entering the country. Approximately 3 percent were age 12 or younger. Some of these children were seeking to escape violence perpetrated by Mexico's drug cartels and associated street gangs.

But the dream of a more prosperous future remains the principal reason most Mexican immigrants—legal as well as undocumented—look to the north. Despite economic improvements, half of Mexico's people remain poor, many of them desperately so. Working in the United States offers the prospect of a better standard of living—even for an undocumented immigrant being paid less than the federal minimum wage ($7.25 per hour in 2015). Mexico's federal minimum wage in 2015 was the equivalent of about $5.00 per day.

Some Mexicans who come to the United States intend to stay permanently. Others, however, plan to return to Mexico. Some are trying to support their families in Mexico through difficult economic times by working in the United States and sending money back home. In 2013, according to the World Bank, nearly $22 billion in remittances were sent to Mexico by Mexicans living in the United States. Some undocumented Mexicans find seasonal work in the United States (for example, in landscaping) and return to their homes for part of the year. In recent years, however, moving back and forth across the border has become increasingly difficult as the United States has tightened border security.

Other undocumented Mexicans plan to cross the border illegally just once, working in the United States only as long as it takes to save enough money for a future they envision in Mexico. Such was the case with a married couple named Alejandro and Lourdes, who were profiled in a *National*

Geographic story. The couple saw Alejandro's journey to the United States as an investment in a better life for themselves and their children. "The family had planned the trip seriously," the story noted.

In Mexico, Alejandro had been making 600 pesos a month (about $70) as a car mechanic; from that and with loans from relatives they had saved the equivalent of almost a thousand dollars, some to pay for his bus fare and a fee to a pollero—a guide to get him across the border—and some to keep Lourdes going until the dollars Alejandro made started to flow south.

The long-term goal was to save enough money so they could open a small business, probably a car repair shop, in Mexico City.

"That is our dream," Lourdes said. "To tell the truth, if he were just working here that dream could not come true. Never."

 # Text-Dependent Questions

1. What does NAFTA stand for?
2. Who were the Zapatistas? What did they want?
3. What was significant about Mexico's 2000 presidential election?

 # Research Project

The Mexican Revolution helped spur a wave of immigration to the United States. Read about the 1910 revolution and its chaotic aftermath. Then draw up a timeline.

3 IMMIGRATION TO THE NORTH

Until the second half of the 20th century, Mexican immigrants passed through a fairly open border to *El norte*, "the North." Illegal migration was not a major issue, most likely because the majority of Mexicans did not stay long in the United States. They traveled to jobs as seasonal workers and then returned home.

The Bracero Program

In early 1942, as large numbers of American men were mobilized to fight in World War II, California farmers predicted that they wouldn't have enough laborers to harvest their crops in the fall. They suggested that Mexican farmworkers be brought to the United States.

After some negotiation, the U.S. and Mexican governments agreed on the establishment of a guest worker program for Mexican agricultural laborers. It was known informally as the Bracero Program (bracero is a Spanish term meaning laborer). Under the program, Mexican laborers signed contracts and were issued temporary work permits. The contracts ran for no longer than a single growing season, after which the braceros had to surrender their work permits and return to Mexico. The braceros' transportation costs were paid, and they were prom-

◄ Some individuals will go to great lengths to live and work in the United States; in this case a Mexican man has sewn himself in the back seat of a van in an attempt to evade border officials. The U.S. Bureau of Customs and Border Protection (BCBP), a branch of the Department of Homeland Security, is responsible for preventing and uncovering such attempts to unlawfully enter the country.

ised decent housing and a small food allowance. They were also legally guaranteed the same wage an American doing identical work would receive. This was a major enticement for braceros, who could earn far more in the United States than they would in Mexico. It was also an assurance for American laborers that growers wouldn't use the braceros to drive down their wages.

In 1942 just 4,200 Mexican workers entered the United States under the Bracero Program. The following year, however, the number jumped to more than 44,000. In 1944 it peaked at over 62,000, declining to around 44,000 in 1945 and 1946. The braceros worked primarily in California and Texas.

For many braceros, the experience didn't turn out the way they'd hoped. Often their living quarters were crowded and unsanitary, and many workers fell ill. Often braceros returned to Mexico with considerably less money than they'd anticipated—the result of being overcharged for basic products at grower-operated stores.

At the end of 1947, with millions of American soldiers having returned to civilian life, the wartime Bracero Program was officially ended. However, many American growers still wanted Mexican laborers to work their fields, and the U.S. government was responsive. For its part, the Mexican government believed that the guest worker program benefited Mexico economically. So the Bracero Program was continued, with some adjustments, until 1964.

In the postwar years, the number of Mexicans participating in

 Words to Understand in This Chapter

bracero—a Mexican laborer, especially one admitted to the United States under contract as a seasonal farmworker.

El norte—Spanish for "the North"; usually refers to the United States.

port of entry—a place where a person may legally enter a country.

electorate—the sum total of voters in an election.

the Bracero Program each year grew dramatically. During the latter half of the 1950s, more than 400,000 braceros were entering the United States annually. By the time the Bracero Program ended in 1964, a total of about 4.6 million Mexicans had entered the United States legally as temporary agricultural workers.

Operation Wetback

On both sides of the border, however, there were incentives to sidestep the legally sanctioned process. In Mexico, laborers who wanted a bracero contract typically had to bribe a local government official to get on a recruitment list. In the United States, some growers didn't want to pay braceros' transportation costs. Ultimately, many Mexicans chose to enter the United States without proper documents, and they found growers who were willing to hire them. It's estimated that, during the 22-year history of the Bracero Program, the number of Mexican farmworkers who came to the United States illegally was about the same as the number who came legally.

By the early 1950s, some Americans—particularly in California and the Southwest—were expressing alarm at the rise in illegal immigration from Mexico. One common complaint was that the presence of undocumented Mexican laborers suppressed wages for American farmworkers. President Harry S. Truman appointed the Commission on Migratory Labor to study the issues. It concluded that American farm wages were indeed being kept low by growers who hired illegal workers. The commission recommended that any growers who knowingly hired illegal workers be fined. Truman endorsed that recommendation, but agricultural interests succeeded in convincing Congress not to enact it.

In 1954, under President Dwight D. Eisenhower, the United States launched Operation Wetback, a program to round up and deport undocumented migrants. (Wetback is an ethnic slur for an illegal Mexican immigrant; the term refers to how the immigrant crosses the border by swimming or wading the Rio Grande.) The U.S. Immigration and Naturalization Service (INS) estimated that about 3.8 million undocumented Mexican immigrants were expelled from the United States between 1954 and 1957.

The INS declared the Eisenhower administration's deportation program an unqualified success. But many historians today consider it a shameful episode. They note that some U.S. citizens of Mexican ancestry were swept up and sent to Mexico in the Operation Wetback dragnet. In addition, deported migrants often weren't treated humanely. They were packed like livestock into trucks, buses, trains, and ships and transported into Mexico, frequently to be abandoned in remote areas with no food or water. A significant number died. Historian Mae Ngai describes a deadly incident in her book *Impossible Subjects*:

> Some 88 braceros died of sun stroke as a result of a round-up that had taken place in 112-degree heat, and [an American labor official] argued that more would have died had Red Cross not intervened. At the other end of the border, in Nuevo Laredo, a Mexican labor leader reported that "wetbacks" were "brought [into Mexico] like cows" on trucks and unloaded fifteen miles down the highway from the border, in the desert.

The 1986 Immigration Reform and Control Act

During the 1960s, the number of legal Mexican immigrants to the United States totaled approximately 430,000. The following decade that figure grew to more than 680,000.

At the same time, the numbers of undocumented Mexican immigrants entering the country also rose steadily. By 1970 it was estimated that more than 750,000 Mexicans were living in the United States illegally.

Concerns about illegal immigration led in 1986 to Congress passing, and President Ronald Reagan signing, the Immigration Reform and Control Act (IRCA)—a law that sought to reduce illegal immigration by making it more difficult for undocumented immigrants to obtain employment. For the first time, an immigration law penalized employers who knowingly hired undocumented workers. Employers were required to check the personal documents—passports, driver's licenses, or birth certifi-

In 1986, U.S. President Ronald Reagan signed the Immigration Reform and Control Act, which tightened restrictions on employers of undocumented Mexican immigrants and gave amnesty to certain undocumented immigrant groups, including those living in the U.S. before 1982.

cates—of potential employees that indicate legal status. Employers who did not comply with the IRCA were subject to fines and possible prison sentences.

While authorizing more resources for law enforcement, the act also included an amnesty program for immigrants, pardoning certain groups of undocumented immigrants living in the United States and enabling them to obtain legal status. Amnesty was available to those who had lived in the United States since January 1, 1982, and agricultural laborers who worked at least 90 days between May 1, 1985, and May 1, 1986.

More than 3 million undocumented immigrants, including approximately 2 million Mexicans, took advantage of the program before it ended in May 1988. Many other Mexican immigrants who were eligible did not apply for amnesty, either because they did not know about the amnesty, lacked proof of residency (such as rental receipts) or employment (such as paycheck stubs), or received improper advice. Under the Legal Immigration Family Equity (LIFE) Act passed by Congress in 2000, tens of thousands of individuals who filed a class-action suit claiming the INS improperly advised them of their eligibility for the amnesty were given a chance to have their cases decided on an individual basis.

Immigration Policy and Politics

In the years following the passage of the IRCA, legal immigration from Mexico increased, in part because once granted legal status, formerly illegal Mexican immigrants had the right to petition for their spouses and children to join them. However, the 1986 legislation did not establish new or sufficient mechanisms for Mexicans to come into the United States and work temporarily with legal status. The insufficient number of legal temporary visas for full-time work, combined with the continuing economic problems in Mexico and the growing demand for labor in the United States, led to an acceleration of illegal immigration. Between 1990 and 1994, more than 1.6 million Mexican undocumented immigrants are estimated to have moved to the United States. Between 1995 and 1999, the figure had risen to 2.9 million.

Mexican immigrants typically cross the border from one Mexican town to its sister city on the U.S. side. There are several sister towns between the 2,000-mile border stretching from California to Texas.

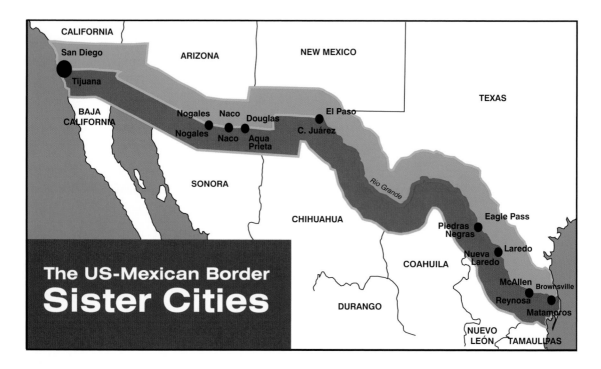

INS enforcement efforts, including raids on factories and farms suspected of employing undocumented workers, were inconsistent and ultimately had little effect on the overall situation. The population of Mexicans living in the United States without authorization continued to rise.

In 1994 a different approach to stopping illegal immigration was attempted in California. A ballot initiative, Proposition 187, was put before the Golden State's voters. If passed, Proposition 187 would prevent undocumented immigrants from accessing public services, such as health care and public education. Supporters said that California taxpayers were footing a $3 billion per year bill to provide public services to the undocumented, with education accounting for about half the total. Republican governor Pete Wilson, who was running for reelection, made Proposition 187 and its anti-immigrant message a major part of his campaign platform. One of his ads showed Mexicans illegally crossing the border with a voiceover warning: "They just keep coming."

Proposition 187 passed easily, with 59 percent voting in favor and 41 percent against. However, the measure was later struck down as unconstitutional by a federal court. Many political analysts credited the measure for helping Wilson win reelection as governor. At the same time, Proposition 187 was widely viewed as having hurt the reputation of the Republican Party in California—and perhaps elsewhere—among the growing bloc of Hispanic voters.

In the years since Proposition 187, the importance of Hispanic voters has grown enormously—and the Republican Party has seemed increasingly incapable of connecting with those voters. In the 1996 presidential election, Hispanics made up just 5 percent of the electorate. By 2012 that proportion had doubled, to 10 percent. The 2012 Republican presidential nominee, Mitt Romney, won just 27 percent of the Hispanic vote, helping guarantee President Barack Obama's reelection. In early 2013, the Republican National Committee issued a report that suggested Romney had alienated Latinos by saying that he wanted

undocumented immigrants to "self-deport." The report said the Republican Party needed to improve its standing among Hispanic voters in order to win future elections. Yet during the campaign for the 2016 Republican presidential nomination, front-runner Donald Trump demonized Mexican immigrants. "When Mexico sends its people [to the United States]," Trump claimed, "they're not sending their best. . . . They're sending people that have lots of problems, and they're bringing those problems [here]. They're bringing drugs. They're bringing crime. They're rapists."

During the 2016 election, Republican candidates like Donald Trump (above) and Ted Cruz (opposite) made immigration reform a central element of their campaigns.

Policing the Border

The presumed need to secure the border with Mexico was a major issue in the 2016 presidential campaign, particularly among candidates seeking the Republican nomination. The discussion at a Republican presidential debate in September 2015 was typical. "The border's been insecure for 25 years," former business executive Carly Fiorina asserted. Retired neurosurgeon Ben Carson suggested that border security was the single most important issue facing the nation. "If we don't seal the border," Carson said, "the rest of this stuff clearly doesn't matter." Senator Ted Cruz claimed he knew what was needed. "How do you secure the borders?" Cruz asked. "Well, I've been leading the fight in the Senate to triple the Border Patrol, to put in place fencings and walls, to put in place a strong biometric exit/entry system." Trump advocated the building of a wall that would run the entire length of the U.S.-Mexico border.

A Pew Research Center poll conducted in September 2015 showed Americans about evenly divided on whether a fence should be erected along the length of the border. In the poll, 46 percent favored the idea, while 48 percent opposed it.

Many Americans were unaware of the steps their government had already taken to increase security at the border. As of 2015, fences lined more than a third of the 1,989-mile (3,200-km) U.S.-Mexico land boundary. In 2015 the Department of

Homeland Security requested nearly $13 billion for Customs and Border Protection. In 2002, by comparison, only $5 billion had been allocated for those functions. While there were slightly under 8,600 U.S. Border Patrol agents in 2000, by 2015 that number stood at about 21,000. Those agents patrol the border in trucks and helicopters, on horseback and quad bikes to prevent illegal crossings. In desert areas they may drag car tires to smooth the sand, making it easier to spot footprints. In other areas seismic sensors buried under roads or along well-traveled paths detect the sound of footsteps. Floodlights illuminate

A section of the border wall between the United States and Mexico. This part of the fence is located in California.

fences, and infrared cameras track movements of anyone trying to slip across the border in the darkness. Drones circle overhead constantly.

While unlawful border crossings may receive a good deal of attention, more than 800,000 people travel back and forth across the U.S.-Mexican border through legal ports of entry every day. Whether walking or driving across, all must present their documents to agents staffing the primary inspection booths at each port of entry. Those who drive often wait in long lines of traffic to present their documents at the inspections station and have their vehicle checked to ensure the driver is not smuggling goods or people.

Most Mexicans enter the United States from one of the Mexican border towns to its sister city on the U.S. side. These sister cities dot the border, beginning at the Pacific in Tijuana, Mexico, and San Diego, California, and stretching to the Gulf of Mexico in Matamoros, Mexico, and Brownsville, Texas.

The San Ysidro port of entry, which separates the booming industrial city of Tijuana from San Diego, is the busiest land crossing in the world. Every day, some 300,000 people go from Mexico to the United States, and from the United States to Mexico, through San Ysidro's inspection station. Some make the trip for their job or for other commercial reasons; others are tourists.

East of San Diego lies Calexico, a small town across the border from the much larger city of Mexicali, Mexico, the state capital of Baja California. An important industrial center featuring a number of maquiladoras on its outskirts, Mexicali attracts millions of Mexicans in search of jobs, some of whom are later drawn to the United States.

Further east in Arizona are four major border towns: Yuma, opposite San Luis, Mexico; Nogales, across from its Mexican namesake, Nogales; Naco, opposite Naco, Mexico (whose name comes from the last two letters of Arizona and Mexico); and Douglas, across from Agua Prieta, Mexico.

A 90-minute drive south of Tucson, Nogales is the busiest

border-crossing station in Arizona and the second-largest point of entry for shipped produce. A story in *Government Executive* magazine described the sophisticated camera system at the crossing in Nogales. "The cameras provide daily security for our officers and backup in the case of a passenger complaint—we can pull the video up right away and put that complaint to rest and protect the inspectors as well," said Joe Lafata, the port director in Nogales. "It's really a top-notch system. Many of the cameras have tilt-zoom capability. We can actually shoot into some of the hills here and watch the spotters [people paid by smugglers to spy on border-crossing operations] as they're watching us. They're there all the time and every once in a while you get a really nice portrait of them."

During the mid-1990s, Border Patrol enforcement efforts such as Operation Hold the Line and Operation Gatekeeper increased enforcement along traditional smuggling routes into Texas and California. Observers believe these programs encour-

The auto lanes at the Tijuana border crossing surprisingly have extremely short lines on this particular morning. Tijuana, just south of San Diego is the busiest crossing point for Mexican immigrants.

aged smugglers to either attempt less-safe routes into those states or more entries through Arizona. With its easy access to the Pan American Highway, Douglas quickly became the largest entry-way for undocumented immigrants. Its sister city, Agua Prieta, still caters to those looking to make desert crossings; city shops carry plastic water jugs, can openers, and other essential items for the desert traveler. Agua Prieta holds the distinction as the largest staging ground for illegal immigration.

Major towns found along Texas's long border with Mexico include El Paso, opposite Ciudad Juárez, Mexico (the border's largest city); Laredo, across from Nuevo Laredo; McAllen, across from Reynosa; and Brownsville, opposite Matamoros.

Each day, nearly 5,000 trucks rumble across the World Trade Bridge, which spans the Rio Grande between Nuevo Laredo and Laredo. The volume of trucks attests to the thriving commerce between the United States and Mexico.

 ## Text-Dependent Questions

1. Why did the United States start the Bracero Program?
2. What was Proposition 187?
3. Identify the busiest border land crossing in the world. Which two cities are on opposite sides of that crossing?

 ## Research Project

Immigration reform has long been a controversial issue in American politics. Investigate the positions of leading Democrats and leading Republicans. Which side do you agree with? Do you think both sides have valid points? Write a one-page essay on what you think the United States should do about its current immigration system. Remember to support your opinions by citing relevant evidence.

4 Making A New Home

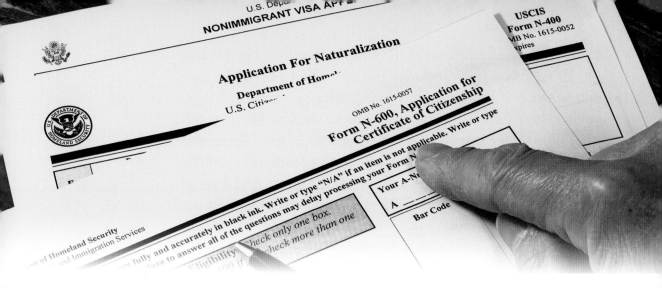

Today, Mexican Americans live in virtually every corner of the country. However, they are concentrated in two regions: the West and the South. In 2011, using data from the U.S. Census Bureau, the Pew Research Center concluded that 52 percent of the 33.7 million people of Mexican origin residing in the United States lived in the West. An additional 35 percent lived in the South.

By a wide margin, California was the state with the most Mexican and Mexican American residents. About 12 million people of Mexican origin were living in the Golden State in 2011. That constituted 32 percent of California's total population. Texas ranked second for Mexican-origin residents, with 8.4 million. One-third of the Lone Star State's total population claimed Mexican ancestry. By themselves, California and Texas are home to more than 6 in 10 Mexicans and Mexican Americans living in the United States. Other states with large Mexican-origin populations include Illinois, Arizona, Florida, Colorado, Nevada, New York, and North Carolina.

Los Angeles County is home to the single largest community of Mexicans and Mexican Americans in the United States. In 2010, according to the U.S. census, some 3.5 million people of

◀A busy street in a Mexican neighborhood, New York City. There are many predominantly Mexican neighborhoods in the United States, some that are still growing every year. The most established of these neighborhoods are in Los Angeles, Chicago, various Texan cities, and New York City, where the Mexican population tripled during the 1990s.

Mexican origin—11 percent of the national total—resided in Los Angeles County, which includes the cities of Los Angeles and Long Beach. San Diego also has a large Mexican American population, as do Tucson, Arizona; Albuquerque, New Mexico; and Dallas and San Antonio, Texas. Outside of the West and Southwest, significant Mexican American populations can be found in New York City, Chicago, Detroit, Denver, and Kansas City. In New York City, the Mexican population tripled during the 1990s, growing from 93,000 in 1990 to nearly 300,000 in 2000. Even Vancouver, Canada, boasts its own "Little Mexico," a Mexican immigrant community located in the heart of the city.

The 1990s saw a trend in which many Mexican immigrants chose to move to small U.S. towns rather than big cities. They were following manufacturing or meat processing plants that relocated from urban areas during the 1980s and 1990s. The small towns and rural areas often prove appealing to new immigrants. Living expenses in these areas can be much lower than in a city. Sometimes the environment is similar to that of the villages immigrants left in rural Mexico.

Hundreds of residents from just one village in Mexico have been known to follow one another to the same town or neighborhood in the United States. The town of East Point, Georgia (2010 population: 33,700), witnessed that migration pattern. East Point became the destination for hundreds of Mexican immigrants from Ejido Modelo, a village located in the state of Jalisco, in western Mexico. Most found work as fabricators at an East Point plant and lived near one another in a tight-knit barrio (a Spanish-speaking section of a town or village). By

 Words to Understand in This Chapter

barrio—a neighborhood of Spanish-speaking residents; from the Spanish word for "suburb" or "township."

segregation—the enforced separation of different racial or ethnic groups in public settings.

A large family of Mexicans sits outside their home in Laredo, Texas. In some cases, the living conditions Mexican immigrants face in U.S. border cities are similar to what they faced in Mexico, but the promise of higher wages persuades them to remain in the United States.

2010, according to the U.S. Census Bureau, 9.5 percent of East Point's residents were of Mexican origin.

Getting a Job

During the latter part of the 1800s and well into the 1900s, many Mexicans crossed the border to work temporary agricultural jobs as migrant laborers. They traveled to farms or orchards, where they harvested crops, then returned home at the end of the growing season. Migrant workers picked cotton in Texas or harvested grapes on large farm estates in California's

Central Valley. The work was hard and low-paying, but still provided more income than was possible to earn in Mexico. As the U.S. economy became industrialized, workers also found jobs with railroad and mining companies.

Early migrant workers found jobs by paying a labor agent to connect them with farms or ranches in need of workers. However, during the 1970s, as more and more Mexican immigrants found jobs that weren't in the agricultural sector, new immigrants came to depend increasingly on friends and families for job advice. Because most of these jobs were in service and manufacturing industries, which tend to be located in or near urban areas, more Mexicans gravitated to the cities where friends and families had already settled. By the early 1990s, most Mexicans lived in or near a city.

If Mexican immigrants now work in a variety of occupations, they still form the backbone of the U.S. agricultural labor

The grape harvest is in full swing in Kern County, California, where farm workers—many from Mexico—pick, sort, cull and pack grapes for distribution to markets.

Sharing the Paycheck with Family Back Home

Over the years, Mexican citizens working in the United States have channeled billions of their hard-earned dollars into Mexico's economy. Many Mexican immigrants regularly send part of each pay-check home to family members. Such transactions are called remittances. During the 1990s, Mexican immigrants supplemented their relatives' incomes by more than
$4.5 billion.

The cash continued to flow at an even greater rate with the new millennium. In the year 2000 Mexican immigrants sent home $6 billion (about $17 million a day). By 2013, remittances totalled more than $20 billion. About one of every five families in Mexico receives money from a relative or relatives abroad.

These financial contributions of Mexican immigrants in the United States to family members back home have become Mexico's second-largest source of foreign revenue, surpassed only by oil.

force. According to the U.S. Department of Agriculture, about two-thirds of the laborers who harvest America's crops today were born in Mexico.

Other Support

Several Mexican American organizations offer information, programs, and various kinds of assistance to Mexican immigrants, including the Mexican American Legal Defense and Educational Fund (MALDEF), the National Council of La Raza, and the American GI Forum, which was founded by Dr. Hector P. García after World War II. García was inspired to start the American GI Forum, which has approximately 50,000 members today, after a Texas funeral home refused to rebury Félix Longoria, a decorated veteran of World War II, because he was Mexican.

One of the earliest groups, the League of United Latin American Citizens (LULAC), was founded in 1929. LULAC grew in large part out of a response to the discrimination that Mexican Americans faced at the time. During the 1920s, throughout much of the Southwest region, Mexicans met with the same "whites only" segregation that African Americans were suffering in the South. Restaurant owners would refuse to serve

Mexican customers. Stores and cinemas posted signs that announced "No Mexicans allowed." Mexican children had to attend segregated schools; they and their families were excluded from facilities such as parks, swimming pools, and public buses and trains.

Concerned Mexican Americans organized and fought back through LULAC. The organization filed lawsuits to end segregation in public facilities, lobbied for Mexican American rights, and provided legal assistance to Mexican Americans who had been arrested. In the 1940s, LULAC successfully took legal action against California and Texas school districts to eliminate the segregation of Mexican students.

A Mexican grocer sells fruit at a store in New York City. Since the 1970s, a growing segment of the Mexican workforce has been landing jobs in American and Canadian cities.

Getting a Green Card

Non-U.S. citizens who are eligible can apply for a green card, which grants them permission to live and work indefinitely in the country, although the process of getting the card can take several years. Officially called the Alien Registration Receipt Card Form I-151, the green card was first issued in the 1940s, when it was actually green. In the years that followed, many designs of the card appeared, most often in various shades of blue. With the green card, which is valid indefinitely (unless its owner leaves the United States for more than a year or is jobless for more than six months), foreign residents can live and work anywhere in the United States.

 # Text-Dependent Questions

1. Which U.S. state has the most Mexican American residents? Which state ranks second?
2. Why did many Mexican immigrants move to small towns during the 1990s?
3. What is the League of United Latin American Citizens? When and why was LULAC founded?

 # Research Project

Use online resources to find out: the total population of your state or province; the number of people in your state or province who are Hispanic; and the number of people in your state or province who are of Mexican ancestry. Present your findings in graph or chart form.

5 CHOOSING BETWEEN THE OLD AND THE NEW

Close-knit Mexican communities in the United States have continuously provided a warm welcome for Mexican immigrants, allowing them to hold on to parts of their culture as they have adjusted to a foreign culture and language. Immigrants often name their neighborhoods after the village they came from, or they simply refer to the area as "Little Mexico." Newcomers can feel comfortable in these neighborhoods, knowing they can easily communicate with others who live there.

Long-established Mexican neighborhoods, such as East Los Angeles, East San Jose, and South El Paso, which have existed for many decades, provide a comfortable environment for the newcomer. Businesses offer the same items that are available south of the border. Grocery stores supply tortillas, mole (a spicy sauce), salsa chipotle, and other Mexican foods. Local pharmacies offer medicines from Mexico, including medicinal teas, herbs, and ointments. In hundreds of Mexican neighborhoods, buildings display colorful murals—originally inspired by Mexican artist Diego Rivera—that proclaim pride in Mexico's history and heritage.

◀ A furniture store in a Hispanic neighborhood of Santa Ana, California, advertises for a Valentine's Day sale in Spanish. In this and other Hispanic neighborhoods in U.S. cities, Mexican restaurants, grocery stores, and convenience stores serve as reminders to Mexican newcomers of their homeland.

At home, the Spanish-speaking immigrant can watch a variety of television programs in his or her own language. The two largest Spanish-language networks, Univision and Telemundo, offer telenovelas (soap operas), game shows, dubbed versions of American programs, and well as coverage of the ever popular sport of fútbol (soccer).

Importance of Family

Family ties are strong in Mexican culture, whether in the home country or an American barrio. Most Mexican immigrants teach their children the value of working for the good of the whole family, not just the individual. These strong ties extend to grandparents, aunts, uncles, and cousins as well. Family members help each other whenever possible, financially and emotionally.

Mexican immigrants often socialize with other immigrant families, many of whom came from the same village or region of Mexico. With family and friends they preserve cherished traditions and rituals in celebrating major life events, such as baptisms, weddings, and funerals. Such gatherings and celebrations often feature traditional dishes originating from the family's home in Mexico. Musical entertainment might include the singing of corridos (folk ballads) or performances of mariachi bands (groups playing violins, guitars, and trumpets).

Painter Diego Rivera (1886–1957) was a leading figure of the Mexican mural movement of the 1920s. His work was a source of national pride for Mexicans, and inspired the many Mexican-themed murals that can be found in U.S. cities today.

 Words to Understand in This Chapter

canonize—in the Roman Catholic Church, to officially declare a dead person a saint.

hybrid—a mixture.

median—the middle value in a series of values ranging from lowest to highest.

quinceañera—a Mexican celebration of a girl's 15th birthday.

status quo—the existing social or political order.

Mexicans also observe family anniversaries such as birthdays with traditional food and drink. A special tradition that highlights children's parties is the breaking of the piñata, a papier-mâché or clay pot in the shape of a person or animal that is filled with candy. The piñata is hung from rope, and blindfolded children take turns trying to strike it with a stick and break it open—releasing its delicious contents to the delight of partygoers. A party favorite for many generations in Mexico, piñatas can be found for sale in retail and party stores across America. Families with and without Mexican heritage traditionally include piñatas in birthday celebrations.

A girl's 15th birthday celebration receives special attention in many Mexican households. The quinceañera is a ceremony that can be as elaborate as a wedding, complete with fancy dresses, a sit-down meal, a hired photographer, and traditional or contemporary Mexican and American music. The religious ceremony of the quinceañera takes place in the Catholic Church in a special mass. At that time the girl being honored renews her vow of commitment to the Catholic Church. Afterwards, everyone celebrates with a party. Sometimes the quinceañera takes place in the girl's home. She may be serenaded by a mariachi band's performance of the folk song "Las Mañanitas."

Mariachi bands are common to most Mexican secular and religious holidays, particularly the *quinceañera*, which celebrates a Mexican girl's 15th birthday.

National and Religious Celebrations

Community celebrations also revolve around Mexico's national holidays. Independence Day, observed on September 16, commemorates the date in 1810 that Father Miguel Hidalgo delivered a speech proclaiming the end of Spanish colonial rule. Mexicans and Mexican Americans celebrate with fiestas, parades, folk dancing, and music.

Cinco de Mayo (the fifth of May) is a relatively minor holiday in Mexico. But in the United States it has become a major celebration of Mexican culture—among those of Mexican heritage and other Americans alike. Cinco de Mayo commemorates the 1862 Battle of Puebla, in which a badly outnumbered Mexican force defeated a French invading army.

Independence Day and Cinco de Mayo (the fifth of May) are two popular festivals that are celebrated in Mexican American communities. (Above) A group of men in warrior costume salute with their swords during an Independence Day procession on September 16. The holiday commemorates the day in 1821 Mexico officially declared its freedom from Spanish colonial rule.

For Cinco de Mayo, revelers dress up in French and Mexican military uniforms to reenact the Battle of Puebla in 1862, in which General Benito Juárez led his troops to victory over the French.

Many Mexicans are deeply religious. In their new country Mexican immigrants continue to observe the traditions, ceremonies, and festivals of their strong Roman Catholic faith, the majority religion in Mexico. Family baptisms, First Communions, confirmations, marriages, and funerals take place in the church, as do observances of religious holidays such as Lent and Christmas. Many Catholic parishes located in Hispanic neighborhoods perform masses in Spanish and include traditional Mexican music.

Native American and African beliefs and practices play an important part in Mexican Catholicism, especially festivities celebrating patron saints. Of particular importance to Mexican immigrants across North America is December 12, celebrated as the Feast Day of Our Lady of Guadalupe. The holiday commemorates the appearance of the Virgin Mary to an Aztec Indian peasant, Juan Diego, in 1531. According to the legend, the Virgin filled Diego's cloak with red roses and left her image on the back of his garment. Many Mexicans consider the Virgin of Guadalupe the patron saint of all Mexico, and the spiritual mother of oppressed people. The Basilica de Guadalupe in Mexico City was built on the site where the Virgin Mary is said to have appeared.

Día de los Muertos—the Day of the Dead—is a hybrid of Aztec Indian and Catholic traditions. It's celebrated on November 1 and 2 (the Catholic feasts of All Saints' Day and All Souls' Day, respectively). For Mexicans, the Day of the Dead is a time to commemorate ancestors. The festivities include visits to gravesites, parades, costumes and decorations, and special foods such as candy skulls.

An Aztec Indian dance is performed in front of the Basilica of Our Lady of Guadalupe during the annual Feast Day. The Aztec performance helps practicing Mexicans remember Juan Diego, an Aztec who is said to have been visited by the Virgin Mary in 1531. Mexican communities hold similar celebrations in North America.

Dual Nationality

For years, Mexican immigrants who were naturalized as U.S. citizens forfeited their rights as citizens of Mexico. In 1998 the Mexican government changed this policy, effectively offering dual nationality to the more than 2 million Mexican-born immigrants who, in becoming U.S. citizens, had lost their status as Mexican nationals. When the law went into effect, hundreds of applicants flocked to their local Mexican consulates throughout the United States to apply for the new designation.

For a $12 fee, applicants received an official Declaration of Mexican Nationality, a document that gave its holder economic privileges such as the right to buy and sell property in Mexico (foreigners face certain restrictions) and apply for Mexican identity cards and passports.

The new status eased travel restrictions for many Mexican immigrants when they wanted to travel home. Consuelo LaMonica explained to the *Hispanic Times Magazine*, "We share a deep emotional attachment to Mexico, even though we have been in this country for a long time. . . . Now, with my new dual nationality, I can go back and forth across the border to visit family without a problem."

In Mexico, Catholics celebrate Antorcha Guadalupana, a tradition begun more than 50 years ago in which runners carry a torch from the Basilica de Guadalupe to their home parish or village, calculating their arrival for December 12, in time for the feast day. The Antorcha tradition is also followed in New York City, home to a fast-growing Mexican immigrant population. After a mass at St. Patrick's Cathedral, on Fifth Avenue, runners bear blazing torches through the streets to their local parishes. In 2015, as has become the tradition in recent years, organizers set up a torch relay of some 3,100 miles (4,990 km) that originated at the Basilica de Guadalupe in Mexico City and ended at St. Patrick's Cathedral in New York City.

The Feast Day of Our Lady of Guadalupe traditionally begins with an early morning mass during which churchgoers sing mañanitas, traditional songs of greeting, to the Virgin. Others may carry red roses or images of the Virgin Mary. Afterward fiestas with music and great food spill over to the blocks of Mexican neighborhoods.

This celebration takes on special significance for many Mexican immigrants living north of the border. As one immigrant explained to the *New York Times*, "All Mexicans are more united because we have a day to celebrate here. We are taking this day to tell more people and more people we want to live in the United States with all the rights everybody else has."

Besides meeting the spiritual needs of its parish members, the Catholic Church also provides for the physical well-being of many new immigrants by providing welfare services, referrals to housing authority agencies, and assistance with filling out forms.

About a third of American Catholics are Hispanic, most of them Mexican. The Catholic Church continues to reach out to the Mexican community, as in 2002, when it canonized Juan Diego, whose visions of the Virgin Mary over 500 years ago inspired many Mexican traditions centered on the sacred figure.

Joining American Society

Many scholars consider immigrants to the United States to be assimilated, or a part of American mainstream society, when

A Mexican man (left) is sworn in as a U.S. citizen during a mass naturalization ceremony in Miami, Florida.

they have obtained good English skills, financial security, and U.S. citizenship. By some of these standards, Mexicans have not had as high a rate of assimilation into the United States as some other immigrant groups. Geographic proximity is a main factor affecting those Mexican immigrants who do not pursue naturalization. In other words, those who expect that after a temporary stay they will take the opportunity to return home may choose not to become citizens. This is also true of many Canadian immigrants.

Yet in many cases Mexican immigrants end up remaining in their new home a long time, and still have limited success in assimilating. In surveys for a 2007 Pew Hispanic Center report, 71 percent of Mexican immigrants said they spoke English only a little or not at all. Of all Hispanic immigrant groups, Mexicans were the least likely to be proficient in English. And just 24 percent spoke English exclusively or mainly at work—also the lowest rate among Hispanic immigrant groups. Immigrants who do not learn English have fewer job choices and typically receive low wages. However, the vast majority of U.S.-born children of Mexican immigrants are fluent in English.

In terms of household income, Mexican Americans lag behind many other Hispanic groups in the United States. In 2013, according to the U.S. Census Bureau, the median household income for people of Mexican origin living in the United States stood at $40,000. That ranked 10th among the 14 largest Hispanic-origin groups in the country, and it was significantly lower than the median household income for all Americans ($51,939).

Becoming a Citizen

Immigrants who choose to become citizens of the United States must meet the following criteria: they must be at least 18 years old (minor children can receive citizenship through their parents) and have been a lawful permanent resident for at least five years, or three years if married to a U.S. citizen. In addition, they must be able to speak, read, and write the English language, be familiar with the government and history of the United States, and be of "good moral character." During the naturalization ceremony, participants must swear an oath of loyalty to the United States.

Immigrants to Canada who wish to be naturalized can retain the citizenship of their native country. Candidates for citizenship must be at least 18 years old (minor children can receive citizenship through their parents) and have lived as a legal resident in Canada for at least two of the previous five years. They must be able to understand and speak English or French well and have a basic knowledge of the history, government, and geography of Canada. The naturalization process involves applying to a citizenship court, appearing at a hearing before a citizenship examiner, and participating in a naturalization ceremony.

Second-Generation Mexicans

Often children of Mexican immigrants grow up straddling two worlds, talking with their parents in Spanish at home and speaking English at school. This next generation grows up bilingual—able to speak two languages. They may act as interpreters, helping Spanish-speaking family members deal with educational, medical, or other issues outside their immediate community.

Most Mexican immigrants prefer that their children speak both Spanish and English. But about half of the children of Hispanic immigrants assimilate into the English-speaking community to such an extent that they don't learn to speak Spanish, or they speak it poorly.

As second-generation immigrants grow up speaking English, they tend to accept the values and ideas of the culture around them. Sometimes the children's new ideas and values clash with those of their parents. For instance, there are first-generation parents who do not approve of girls playing sports, a popular school activity in the United States. Children may rebel against adults, ignoring the traditional value of always showing respect to elders. Some extended generations of Mexican families have dropped their allegiance to Roman Catholicism, adopting Protestant faiths instead. However, many Mexican immigrants

Americans participate in a Cinco de Mayo festival in Florida.

want to keep the traditional values of their culture, which at times seem at odds with those of the mainstream American culture.

Mexico's Changing Attitudes Toward Immigration

When President Vicente Fox took office in 2000, one of his first acts was the creation of a special federal agency: the Office for Mexicans Living Abroad. The new department represented the interests of approximately 20 million legal and illegal Mexican immigrants living in the United States.

The official recognition given to immigrants reflected a change of heart for the Mexican government, which for years had held a rather conflicted view of citizens who packed up and moved to "El norte." On the one hand, Mexican officials understood that their country couldn't create enough jobs for its own people. The U.S. labor market served as a kind of social safety

valve, absorbing Mexican workers who would otherwise be unemployed and discontent with the status quo. Moreover, remittances from Mexicans living and working in the United States significantly alleviated poverty in Mexico. On the other hand, the Mexican government had a tendency to reproach immigrants for abandoning their home country.

President Fox, however, praised Mexican immigrants as "national heroes." He pointed out their "courage, determination, perseverance and valor," as evidenced by their accomplishments in America. Mexicans living in the United States reacted positively to the attention. The Office for Mexicans Living Abroad closed within two years, though, and its duties were absorbed by the Ministry of Foreign Relations and the Mexican consulates in the United States.

After he became Mexico's president in 2012, Enrique Peña Nieto made improving the plight of undocumented Mexican immigrants a priority. Peña Nieto called on the United States to

Unable to convince Congress to pass immigration reforms, President Barack Obama issued executive orders that would affect Mexican immigrants.

enact comprehensive immigration reform. However, that was a hot-button political issue in the United States, and Congress failed to pass immigration-reform legislation.

But President Barack Obama issued several executive orders that affected many Mexican immigrants in the country without authorization. In June 2012, Obama announced a policy called Deferred Action for Childhood Arrivals (DACA). Persons who'd entered the country illegally before the age of 16, who'd lived in the country continuously since June 2007 (later changed to January 1, 2010), and who fulfilled certain other requirements could qualify under DACA.

In November 2014, President Obama announced another policy, Deferred Action for Parents of Americans and Lawful Permanent Residents, or DAPA. Under DAPA, undocumented immigrants who'd lived in the United States continuously since January 1, 2010, and who had children who were U.S. citizens or lawful permanent residents would be exempt from deportation. They could also receive a renewable three-year work permit. However, several states filed lawsuits over DAPA, and in February 2015 a federal court halted the implementation of DAPA pending the outcome of those suits.

 Text-Dependent Questions

1. What is a quinceañera?
2. What event does Cinco de Mayo commemorate?
3. What is DACA?

 Research Project

If you are of Mexican heritage, write about how your family celebrates a traditional holiday, or about a specific celebration that was particularly memorable for you. If you aren't of Mexican heritage, research a traditional Mexican holiday and write a one-page report.

6 Problems Facing Mexican Immigrants

While legal Mexican immigrants face many difficulties in America, far greater problems await undocumented immigrants, many of whom risk their lives attempting to enter the country by crossing the border illegally.

Deadly Border Crossings

Between 1998 and 2013, according to figures from the U.S. Border Patrol, nearly 7,000 people died trying to get into the United States from Mexico. The actual death toll, however, is probably considerably higher. The Tucson-based Colibrí Center for Human Rights, which attempts to account for people missing along the U.S.-Mexico border, has more than 1,500 open cases in Arizona alone. But the bodies of some would-be migrants who perish in remote areas may never be found.

For the undocumented, attempting to enter the United States from Mexico has become more perilous in recent years. In 1998, according to the Border Patrol, 263 people died crossing the border. By 2012—even as an abundance of evidence indicated that the number of attempted crossings was way down—fatalities reached 477. Deaths fell slightly the following year, to 445, according to Border Patrol statistics.

The rise in migrant fatalities along the U.S. southern border

◀ An unmarked burial site in San Diego for unidentified Mexicans who died trying to illegally enter the U.S. Undocumented immigrants often rely on smugglers known as coyotes for help, though typically these profiteers have little concern for the immigrants' safety.

has been attributed primarily to changes in Border Patrol enforcement. Previously, a large portion of the undocumented attempted to cross the border from one urban area to another: for example, from Tijuana to San Diego; Nogales, Mexico, to Nogales, Arizona; or Ciudad Juárez to El Paso, Texas. But beginning in the 1990s, the United States made it more difficult to cross in those areas with the construction of fences, the use of high-tech detection equipment such as motion sensors, and the deployment of additional Border Patrol officers. As a result, illegal migrants increasingly attempted to cross the border in rugged and remote areas, including desert land. In those areas, migrants have succumbed to dehydration, heat stroke, and exposure.

A sign warns motorists to watch out for immigrants crossing the highway. These signs have become a necessity in San Diego, where hundreds of immigrants have been struck and killed by cars.

"It's a humanitarian crisis," notes Enrique Morones, executive director of Border Angels, an immigrant advocacy group, "and it's been a humanitarian crisis since 1994 [the year the

 Words to Understand in This Chapter

coyote—in the context of immigration, a smuggler paid to guide illegal immigrants across the Mexico-U.S. border.

microbe—a microorganism (such as a bacterium or virus), especially one that causes disease.

pollo—Spanish word for "chicken"; in the context of immigration, refers to a coyote's customer.

United States started constructing border fences]. Before that wall was being built, one or two people would die every month. After the wall was built, you started having one or two per day."

Many undocumented Mexicans believe their odds of successfully getting into the United States are better if they hire a smuggler, known as a "coyote," to guide them on foot across the border or to conceal them in vehicles traveling north. Coyotes recruit their customers, or pollos (literally, "chickens" in Spanish), at bus stops, public parks, plazas, and hotels in Mexican border towns, often charging a couple thousand dollars or more per person. Sometimes the coyote employs others: a vendepollo (chicken seller) to recruit clients, a brincador (jumper) to lead the migrants across the border, and a driver to deliver them to a safe house. After payment is made (often wired

Officers with U.S. Immigration and Customs Enforcement (ICE) detain immigrants in Houston who are suspected of being in the country illegally. ICE was formed to enforce federal laws governing border control, customs, trade and immigration to promote homeland security and public safety.

by a relative already living in the United States), the undocumented immigrant can leave for his or her final destination.

Coyotes have a well-deserved reputation for callousness. Many have been known to abandon their charges without food or water in the desert. Others have led their customers to bandits who prey on the hapless migrants.

Migrants who are transported by truck or van don't necessarily fare better than those who travel on foot. Coyotes have been known to pack as many as 40 people, without food or water, into the back of a truck. As the vehicle heats up during the journey along desert roads, the occupants crammed inside its metal walls are susceptible to heat exhaustion. To pass safely through highway checkpoints, smugglers sometimes force immigrants from a truck, promising they will be met further down the highway. Then the truck may never show up at the designated meeting point, or, worse, the undocumented immigrants become lost in the desert.

A Mexican girl wades through the sewage-filled New River to cross the border into Calexico, California. By entering the river, immigrants risk exposing themselves to a number of infections and diseases.

Death and Disease

The rivers separating Mexico and the United States have proven deadly for many undocumented immigrants, who have drowned while trying to cross the Rio Grande to Texas or the All-American Canal to California. Other undocumented immigrants suffer serious infections and disease resulting from wading through the sewage-filled New River, which flows north from Mexicali to the Salton Sea at the California border. A vast repository of agricultural and industrial waste, the river contains microbes that cause a variety of illnesses, ranging from hepatitis A to cholera. It is considered one of the most polluted rivers in the United States.

The Tijuana–San Diego crossing had been the border's most heavily trafficked crossing site before Operation Gatekeeper funneled traffic to the east in the mid-1990s. So many undocumented immigrants were crossing along Interstate 5 in San Diego that the state of California put up yellow caution signs. Each sign—featuring the figures of a running man, woman, and child—indicates places on the freeway where drivers need to watch out for migrants who have just crossed the border. Despite the warning signs, hundreds of people have been struck and killed over the years.

Bilingual Education and ESL

During the mid-1900s, Latino advocates pushed to change public school systems, encouraging them to offer programs that would let Spanish-speaking children learn in their native language. As early as the 1930s and 1940s one educator, George Isidore Sanchez (1906–72), sought educational reforms. One important reform in particular was the establishment of bilingual instruction for Spanish-speaking children. But it was not until the Chicano movement of the 1960s that some of his ideas about using Spanish-speaking teachers and studying the contributions of Mexican Americans were put into practice.

In 1968 Congress passed the Bilingual Education Act, which provided federal funds to public schools for programs taught in

the Spanish language. School districts could use the money to hire bilingual teachers and materials for teaching children who did not speak English as their first language.

Teachers of bilingual-education classes in Hispanic communities taught English-language skills while presenting curriculum content (such as math, science, social studies, and language arts) in Spanish. Later, students could transition into classes taught only in English. Another form of bilingual education brings together Spanish-speaking and English-speaking students, who together take some subjects in Spanish and others in English. This way each ethnic group learns the other's language.

Many schools rely on the English as a Second Language (ESL) program, in which Spanish-speaking and other foreign students attend one or more classes where they practice speaking and writing English or are taught curriculum subjects in their native tongue. For the rest of the school day, these students return to the mainstream, English-speaking classes.

Since the 1960s, bilingual education has been controversial. Many school districts have complained about having to pay

An English as a Second Language (ESL) class for adults, located in Los Angeles. Language instruction for younger Hispanic students has been a debated issue for years in the U.S.; school leaders clash the most over how and when Hispanic students should begin receiving instruction in English.

additional costs for bilingual programs, but a 1974 decision by the United States Supreme Court ruled that public schools had to provide for students who did not speak English as their native language. In the 1980s, however, the federal government cut funds for the program. Over the years several states, including Arizona and California, passed laws banning the program in public schools.

Education researchers disagree about the effectiveness of bilingual education. Supporters claim it would be more effective if properly funded. Opponents say that children would readily learn English and that compelling them to learn in Spanish holds them back in a society where speaking English is a crucial job qualification.

In 1998 California voters approved Proposition 227, an initiative that banned bilingual education in the state's public schools and replaced it with an English immersion program, which required students speaking a foreign language to learn in

Many Mexican immigrants travel back and forth between the United States and their homeland, and a significant portion of the immigrant population eventually moves back to Mexico for good. This is the pedestrian border crossing station at San Ysidro.

an all-English environment. The measure was immediately challenged. But in October 2002, a federal appeals court upheld the initiative, and the ban remained in place. Since then, however, some California school districts have turned to "dual immersion" programs, in which English and one other language are used daily in every facet of instruction—for all students, not just those whose families aren't native English-speakers.

Returning Home

Unlike immigrants to the United States from, say, Asia or Europe, Mexican Americans can visit their native land relatively easily. For undocumented Mexicans, however, the risk of being apprehended at the border is always a concern. But once a Mexican immigrant has a green card, or lawful permanent resident status, he or she can go back and forth between the United States and Mexico freely. Many legalized immigrants return home to celebrate Christmas holidays, for summer visits, or for

Many law-abiding immigrants want to remain in the United States, where they have established better lives for themselves and their families, but fear that they may be deported if they do not have the proper documentation.

special celebrations, such as las fiestas patronales. These festivals, often lasting a week or more, honor the patron saints of Mexican villages.

In recent years, many Mexicans living in the United States have decided to move back to Mexico. According to the 2014 Mexican National Survey of Demographic Dynamics, one million Mexican immigrants and their families—including U.S.-born children—returned to Mexico between 2009 and 2014. During the same period, U.S. Census Bureau estimates indicate that just 875,000 Mexican nationals left Mexico to come to the United States. Economics played a part in this net outflow of migrants from the United States: Following the Great Recession of 2007–09, the U.S. labor market remained poor. But 61 percent of the Mexicans who left the United States said their primary reason for doing so was to be reunited with family in Mexico, according to the Mexican National Survey of Demographic Dynamics. Meanwhile, 14 percent said they'd been deported from the United States.

 ## Text-Dependent Questions

1. Deaths of undocumented immigrants trying to cross the southern border into the United States rose sharply after the 1990s. What is believed to have caused that rise?

2. What did California's Proposition 227 ban?

3. What are las fiestas patronales?

 ## Research Project

To become a U.S. citizen, an immigrant from another country must pass a civics test. U.S. Citizenship and Immigration Services offers practice tests at: https://my.uscis.gov/prep/test/civics/view
Take a test. What percentage did you get correct? Do some further research about any answers you got wrong.

7 OUTLOOK FOR THE MEXICAN AMERICAN COMMUNITY

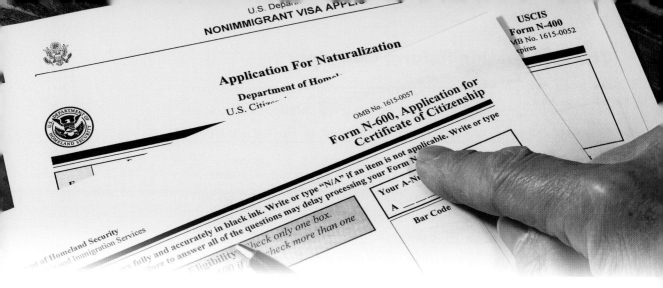

Each U.S. census since 1970 has recorded steady growth in the foreign-born population. In 1970 the census counted 9.6 million U.S. residents who were born in a foreign country. That constituted 4.7 percent of the total U.S. population. By 1980 the number of foreign-born residents had climbed to 14.1 million (6.2 percent of the U.S. population); by 1990, to 19.8 million (7.9 percent); and by 2000, to 31.1 million (11.1 percent). In 2010, the number of foreign-born residents stood at 40 million—12.9 percent of the total population, or about one in every eight people in the United States.

Mexico is by far the largest country of origin for the U.S. foreign-born population. In 2010, according to the Census Bureau, 11.7 million people born in Mexico were living in the United States. That was more than five times the next-closest country of origin, China, in which were born 2.2 million U.S. residents.

About half of the Mexican-born residents of the United States are undocumented immigrants, according to 2015 estimates by the Pew Research Center. The need for immigration reform is clear. But achieving the necessary political consensus on the issue has proved elusive.

◀ Seasonal farm workers pick strawberries in the Salinas Valley of California.

The Immigration Reform Quandary

Several factors explain why attempts to comprehensively reform the U.S. immigration system have foundered. Some involve competing policy objectives. Others have more to do with partisan politics.

Any comprehensive immigration reform must account for the estimated 11.3 million people already living in the country without authorization. Some immigration hard-liners—including 2016 Republican presidential candidate Donald Trump—have called for the deportation of all illegal immigrants. But policy analysts generally agree that, even if such a program were desirable, it wouldn't be feasible. The resources needed to locate, detain, and then transport out of the country more than 11 million people—roughly the population of New York City and Chicago combined—would be prohibitive.

Yet many Americans—conservative political leaders and ordinary citizens alike—chafe at the idea of granting undocumented immigrants legal status. That, they say, wouldn't be fair to all the people who want to move to the United States but go through the legal—and often lengthy—process of obtaining a green card. Additionally, any amnesty for undocumented immigrants could have the effect of encouraging more illegal immigration. That is widely believed to have occurred as a result of the 1986 Immigration Reform and Control Act, because new undocumented migrants assumed they too would eventually be granted legal status.

 Words to Understand in This Chapter

delegation—a body of representatives; a group of persons chosen to represent others.

demographer—a specialist in the study of human populations, including their size, growth, density, and distribution.

wage theft—the illegal underpayment or nonpayment of wages due a worker.

But the presence of millions of people "living in the shadows" of U.S. society also produces undesirable consequences. Because they fear deportation, undocumented immigrants tend to be reluctant to report abuses. In the workplace, this makes them susceptible to exploitation—including wage theft and the flouting of safety regulations—by unscrupulous employers. Certain sectors of the U.S. economy, especially agriculture, are highly dependent on low-wage workers. But the availability of undocumented workers may suppress wages generally for workers in those sectors. That's one reason labor unions such as the AFL-CIO have come out in support of immigration reform and legalization for the undocumented.

In recent years, the issue of immigration has increasingly divided America's two major political parties. President George W. Bush, a Republican, made a push for comprehensive immigration reform—including a "pathway to citizenship" for undocumented immigrants—during his second term in office.

President Bush signs the Enhanced Border Security and Visa Entry Reform Act with congressional members in attendance, May 2002. The act, along with the USA PATRIOT Act, was passed in response to the September 2001 terrorist attacks.

Democrats in Congress were largely supportive. But Republican opposition quashed a 2007 immigration bill that had been introduced in the Senate. "The message is crystal-clear," said Senator David Vitter, a Republican from Louisiana. "The American people want us to start with enforcement at the border and at the workplace and don't want promises. They want action, they want results, they want proof, because they've heard all the promises before."

In the years that followed, Republicans would insist on increased border security and stepped-up enforcement against undocumented immigrants as preconditions to any possible immigration reform plan. Democrats, on the other hand, tended to emphasize the need to confer some form of legal status on the large undocumented population.

To the surprise of many observers, deportations of undocumented immigrants rose under President Barack Obama, a Democrat. In 2008, the last year of Bush's presidency, 360,000 immigrants were deported, according to the Department of Homeland Security. In 2009, the first year of Obama's presidency, that number shot up to 392,000. In 2012, deportations totaled 418,000. Meanwhile, the number of Border Patrol agents increased, from 17,499 in 2008, to 20,119 in 2009, to 21,394 in 2012. At the same time, apprehensions of undocumented migrants at the border declined significantly—solid evidence, experts say, that illegal immigration was also slowing.

While Obama called on Congress to pass comprehensive immigration reform, his relationship with Republican lawmakers was strained at best. No legislation emerged.

Reform Sidelined

The political landscape surrounding immigration reform appeared to change with the 2012 election. President Obama won reelection, besting his Republican opponent, Mitt Romney, by 44 percentage points among Hispanic voters. Mainstream Republicans understood that they had a major problem with Latinos, and much of that problem could be traced to the

Senators Charles Schumer of New York and John McCain of Arizona were among the sponsors of the Border Security, Economic Opportunity, and Immigration Modernization Act. The reform legislation passed the Senate with bipartisan support, but died in the House of Representatives.

Republican Party's hard-ine stance on immigration. Party leaders believed that they would have to resolve the immigration issue in order to be competitive among Hispanic voters.

In 2013 a group of four Republican and four Democratic senators crafted a comprehensive immigration reform bill that attempted to strike a balance between security and enforcement and legalization for the undocumented. The bill would provide several billion dollars for the hiring of 3,500 additional Border Patrol agents, the construction of more border fencing, and the deployment of additional surveillance drones. Undocumented immigrants who'd entered the United States before January 1, 2012, would have a pathway to citizenship—but it would be a long one. They'd have to pay a $1,000 fine and any back taxes, learn English, stay employed, and pass a criminal background check in order to apply for a green card. But it would take 10 years before a green card would be issued. Three years after that, the immigrant would be eligible for citizenship. Among other provisions, the bill would also create a small-scale guest worker program.

On June 28, 2013, the Senate passed the Border Security, Economic Opportunity, and Immigration Modernization Act. The vote was 68–32. But conservative Republicans in the House of Representatives objected to any measure that would legalize the undocumented. In the end, John Boehner, the Republican Speaker of the House, refused to bring an immigration bill to a vote.

A Large and Growing Community

Using data from the U.S. Census Bureau, a 2015 report from the Pew Research Center charted the steady rise in the Mexican-origin population of the United States. In 1980, according to the report, there were 8.8 million people of Mexican ancestry (three-quarters of them U.S. born) living in the United States. That accounted for less than 4 percent of the total U.S. population. By 2013 the Mexican-origin population had swelled to 34.6 million (about two-thirds of whom were born in the United States), or nearly 11 percent of the total U.S. population. In other words, more than one of every 10 people living in the United States was born in Mexico or is of Mexican heritage.

Mexicans have been the largest driver of the huge rise in the Hispanic population of the United States. And that rise is expected to continue. Demographers project that by midcentury, at least one-quarter of all Americans will be Hispanic.

But the category "Hispanic" doesn't make a lot of sense to many people who are classified as such. Yes, Hispanics share the Spanish language (albeit with the sorts of national differences that, for example, distinguish American, British, Irish, and Australian forms of English). However, people in the 20 Hispanic countries differ from one another, sometimes markedly. Their countries developed under unique historical circumstances, and that helped shape their cultures in different ways. Even in America's "melting pot," differences between Hispanic groups may endure. In experience and outlook, an average Mexican American family may have little in common with, say, a Cuban American, Salvadoran American, or Argentinian American family.

"Overall," observed Ciro Rodriguez, a former congressman from Texas who served as chairman of the Congressional Hispanic Caucus, "each [Hispanic group] is different in a lot of ways." Rodriguez was born in the Mexican state of Coahuila.

For demographer Robert Ramirez, many of the differences between Hispanic groups in the United States can be explained by the varying circumstances that drove, and in some cases continue to drive, emigration from their country of origin. "There certainly are wide socioeconomic variations that have a lot to do with the historical immigration trends for each group," Ramirez observed.

When compared with other Hispanic groups, U.S. residents of Mexican origin don't fare especially well economically. In 2013, according to the Pew Research Center, Mexican Americans ranked 10th among the 14 largest Hispanic groups in the country in median family income. Their poverty rate (26 percent) was also fifth highest.

The Mexican American population is notably young. Its median age in 2013, according to the Pew Research Center, was 26—lowest among the 14 largest Hispanic groups and more than a decade younger than the median age of Americans overall.

In addition, Mexican American women have a higher fertility rate (as does the Hispanic population generally) than American women as a whole. A Pew survey conducted in 2011 found that 8 percent of Mexican American women age 15–44 had given birth over the previous 12 months. The rate for all American women age 15–44 was 6 percent. Given its youth and higher fertility rate, the Mexican American community is likely to see its share of the overall U.S. population continue to grow in coming decades. And that could very well lead to increased cultural, economic, and political influence.

Cultural Influence

Spanish-language media took off as early as the 1980s, with the success of two major television networks, Univision and Telemundo. In the first quarter of 2015, Univision, headquartered in New York City, ranked as the fifth most-watched U.S. broadcast network in prime time, behind only NBC, CBS, Fox, and ABC. In some markets—such as Los Angeles; Dallas;

A Telemundo news van at the location of a news story in Brooklyn, New York. Telemundo, a Spanish-language television network, and its rival Univision compete with other U.S. networks for Mexican American viewers.

Houston; and Fresno, California—Univision stations were number one in viewership, irrespective of language. Telemundo—which is headquartered near Miami and in San Juan, Puerto Rico—has not enjoyed that level of success but is nonetheless quite popular.

In addition to Spanish-language television, there are hundreds of Spanish-language radio stations broadcasting throughout the country. They reach millions of Hispanic American listeners in total. Newsstands and libraries offer countless selections of Spanish-language newspapers, magazines, and books.

If Spanish-language media abound in the United States, Hispanics generally—and Mexican Americans specifically—are underrepresented in the mainstream media. That was the conclusion of a 2014 study, "The Latino Media Gap: A Report on the State of Latinos in U.S. Media," from Columbia University. According to the Census Bureau, Hispanics constituted 17.4 percent of the U.S. population in 2014. Yet "The Latino Media

Gap" concluded that less than 1 percent of the news coverage in the mainstream media featured Latinos. In 2013 none of the top 10 movies or scripted network TV shows featured any Latino actors in leading roles. The Latino characters that are depicted in mainstream movies or TV shows, the report's authors said, tend to be stereotypes, such as criminals, maids, or unskilled laborers. This may be partly attributable to the dearth of Latinos in creative and executive positions in the film and television industries. As the report noted:

> In the 2010 to 2013 period, Latinos comprised none of the top ten television show creators, 1.1% of producers, 2% of writers, and 4.1% of directors. In top ten movies, Latinos accounted for 2.3% of directors, 2.2% of producers, and 6% of writers. Even more dramatic, no Latinos currently serve as studio heads, network presidents, CEOs, or owners. Among the top 53 television, radio, and studio executives (including chairpersons), only one is Latina.

Consumer pressure might be brought to bear to change this situation. In 2015 Hispanics in the United States represented an estimated $1.6 trillion in purchasing power.

Economic Impact

Many American businesses are tapping into the rapidly growing Hispanic market. Utility companies, banks, and real estate agencies hire bilingual personnel, offer Spanish-language telephone service, and print brochures and pamphlets in both English and Spanish. Many companies specifically target the Hispanic market in television commercials and other forms of advertising. The potential earnings are enormous.

Mexican Americans, too, have been tapping into the Hispanic consumer market. According to the U.S. Census Bureau's Survey of Business Owners (SBO), Mexican Americans owned one million businesses nationwide in 2007. Not surprisingly, a large majority of these businesses (70.5 percent) were located in California and Texas, the states with the biggest Mexican American populations. California had 373,681 Mexican American–owned firms; Texas, 356,706. Combined, their annual receipts topped $95 billion.

According to the SBO, a large majority of businesses owned by Mexican Americans didn't employ anyone besides the owner. Those that did, however, employed a total of 1.1 million workers nationwide, with combined payrolls of $26.7 billion.

A Growing Political Force

The political importance of Mexican Americans is becoming increasingly evident. It's not just that Hispanics are one of the fastest-growing segments of the electorate, and that Mexican Americans constitute about 6 of every 10 eligible Hispanic voters. It's also that certain presidential battleground states—states that either a Democratic or Republican candidate might plausibly win—contain large Mexican American populations. For example, 30 percent of New Mexico's people are of Mexican origin, according to the Pew Research Center. The figure for Arizona is only slightly lower, at 27 percent; for Colorado, it's 16 percent.

In 2012 President Obama won about 78 percent of the Mexican American vote. That was 7 percentage points higher than Obama's margin among Hispanic voters overall. As has historically been the case, however, turnout among Mexican Americans was low. Just 42.2 percent of eligible Mexican American voters cast a ballot. The rate for Cuban Americans, by comparison, was 67.2 percent; for all Americans, turnout was 58.2 percent.

In certain parts of the country, Mexican Americans are already a major political force at the state level. In 2015, for example, more than one-quarter of the members of the Texas House of Representatives were part of the Mexican American Legislative Caucus. That same year, the Texas delegation to the United States Congress included Henry Cuellar and Joaquin Castro. Among Cuellar and Castro's colleagues in the U.S. House of Representatives were Arizona's Raúl Grijalva and California's Loretta Sanchez and Linda Sánchez. Susana Martinez was serving as governor of New Mexico, and Brian

Sandoval was governor of Nevada. All were Mexican Americans.

In the coming decades, these leaders will no doubt be followed by many other Mexican Americans driven to serve their community and their country. Immigrants from Mexico and their descendants have contributed enormously to keeping the United States strong and vibrant—and they'll continue to do so as long as there is a United States.

 ## Text-Dependent Questions

1. Identify some of the major provisions of the Border Security, Economic Opportunity, and Immigration Modernization Act of 2013. What ultimately happened to the bill?

2. Name the two largest Spanish-language TV networks in the United States.

3. About what proportion of Hispanic eligible voters are Mexican American?

 ## Research Project

Choose a Mexican American, past or present, who made a mark in the arts. It could be a painter or sculptor, a musician, an actor, or a writer. Write a one-page biography of your subject, including his or her most important achievements.

Famous Mexican-Americans

JOAN BAEZ (1941–), celebrated singer and guitarist who achieved popularity during the 1960s and '70s; also a political activist and advocate for nonviolent protest.

CÉSAR E. CHÁVEZ (1927–93), activist for migrant workers' rights and social justice for the Latino community; cofounder of the United Farmworkers Union (1962). Awarded the Presidential Medal of Freedom posthumously in 1994; commemorated on U.S. postage stamp in 2003.

LINDA CHAVEZ (1947–), president of the Center for Equal Opportunity, a public policy research organization based in Washington, D.C.; author of Out of the Barrio: Toward a New Politics of Hispanic Assimilation and a political analyst for the TV network Fox.

LINDA CHAVEZ-THOMPSON (1944–), labor leader; national vice-president of the Labor Council for Latin American Advancement between 1986 and 1996; executive vice president of the AFL-CIO.

HENRY G. CISNEROS (1947–), first Mexican American U.S. secretary of housing and urban development (1993–97); served as mayor of San Antonio, Texas (elected in 1981).

SANDRA CISNEROS (1954–), writer of Chicana novels (*The House on Mango Street, Caramelo*), poetry (*My Wicked Wicked Ways*), and short stories (*Woman Hollering Creek and Other Stories*).

ERNESTO GARAZA (1905–84), political activist and scholar specializing in Latin American studies; worked to improve the conditions and treatment of Mexican farm laborers and urban workers; authored Chicano autobiography *Barrio Boy* (1971), the story of his and his family's immigration to the United States.

HENRY B. GONZÁLEZ (1916–2000), first Mexican American to serve in Texas state senate in 100 years (elected in 1956); elected to U.S. House of Representatives, where he served longer than any other Hispanic (1961–98); first Mexican American from Texas in a national office. Cofounded Hispanic Congressional Caucus.

SALMA HAYEK (1968–), acclaimed actress featured in such films as *Desperado* (1995), *Fools Rush In* (1997), *Dogma* (1999), *Frida* (2002), *Grown Ups* (2010) and *Grown Ups 2* (2013). Received Blockbuster Entertainment Award, Favorite Supporting Actress in an Action Film, for *Wild Wild West*, 1999; and Golden

Globe and Oscar nomination for Best Actress in *Frida*, 2002. Nominated for several Emmy Awards for her work as a producer and guest star on the television show *Ugly Betty*.

OSCAR DE LA HOYA (1973–), super welterweight boxer and Olympic gold-medal winner (1992); won ten world championship titles in six different weight classes during his sixteen-year career, which ended in 2009. Now runs a company that promotes boxing matches nationally.

FRANCISCO JIMÉNEZ (1943–), writer and editor of Mexico-themed books for adults and children, including a collection of short stories based on his life: *The Circuit: Stories from the Life of a Migrant Child*.

MARIO MOLINA (1943–), Massachusetts Institute of Technology professor of Earth, Atmospheric, and Planetary Sciences; winner of 1995 Nobel Prize in Chemistry for work in research for atmospheric chemistry, particularly the formation and depletion of ozone in the atmosphere.

GREGORY NAVA (1949–), screenwriter and film director. Acclaimed for the Oscar-nominated film *El Norte* (1984, which relates the story of a Mexican brother and sister who immigrate to the United States). Other directorial films include *Mi Familia/My Family* (1995), *Selena* (1997), *Why Do Fools Fall in Love* (1998), and *Killing Pablo* (2002).

EDWARD JAMES OLMOS (1947–), actor, filmmaker, political activist. Acclaimed in the 1980s for his Emmy Award–winning role on television series *Miami Vice*; nominated for an Oscar for his role in 1988 film *Stand and Deliver*, which tells the true story of a Hispanic math teacher who inspires his students. Starred in the series *Battlestar Galactica* from 2004 to 2009. Director of films including *American Me* (1992) and *Jack and Marilyn* (2002).

DEREK PARRA (1970–), long-track speed skater who became first Mexican American to win a gold medal at the Winter Olympics (2002).

FEDERICO PEÑA (1947–), mayor of Denver, Colorado; U.S. secretary of transportation (1993–97); secretary of energy (1997–98).

SELENA QUINTANILLA PEREZ (1971–95), popular singer born in Lake Jackson, Texas, whose rising career was cut short when she was murdered at age 23; in 1993 *Selena Live* received a Grammy Award for Best Mexican American album. Another Grammy-nominated album, *Amor Prohibido*, was released in 1994.

ANTHONY RUDOLPH OAXACA QUINN (1915–2001), Oscar-winning actor (for *Viva Zapata!* in 1952) who appeared in more than 200 films during a 60-year acting career; remembered for roles in *Zorba the Greek* and *Lawrence of Arabia*.

LINDA RONSTADT (1946–), acclaimed singer; developed a large following during the 1970s and '80s; has recorded 12 platinum and 17 gold albums, including a 1987 album of traditional Mexican and Spanish songs, *Canciones de Mi Padre*.

EDWARD R. ROYBAL (1916–), Congressman from California for more than 30 years (1963–93); cofounded Hispanic Congressional Caucus (1976); first Mexican American since 1881 to win a seat on the Los Angeles City Council (elected in 1949). As member of U.S. House of Representatives, authored first bilingual education bill and fostered legislation to provide access to bilingual proceedings in U.S. courts.

CARLOS SANTANA (1947–), talented guitarist whose recordings of Latin-flavored rock music have charted for decades, beginning with the Santana Blues Band in 1966; winner of ten Grammy Awards; inducted into the Rock and Roll Hall of Fame in 1998.

LUIS VALDEZ (1940–), playwright and film director; called "father of Chicano theater"; founded El Teatro Campesino in 1965, a touring theater troupe that dramatized the plight of migrant farmworkers; writer, producer, and director of plays such as *Zoot Suit* (1978), which was later adapted into a movie; wrote and directed the film *La Bamba* (1987).

Series Glossary of Key Terms

assimilate—to adopt the ways of another culture; to fully become part of a different country or society.

census—an official count of a country's population.

deport—to forcibly remove someone from a country, usually back to his or her native land.

green card—a document that denotes lawful permanent resident status in the United States.

migrant laborer—an agricultural worker who travels from region to region, taking on short-term jobs.

naturalization—the act of granting a foreign-born person citizenship.

passport—a paper or book that identifies the holder as the citizen of a country; usually required for traveling to or through other foreign lands.

undocumented immigrant—a person who enters a country without official authorization; sometimes referred to as an "illegal immigrant."

visa—official authorization that permits arrival at a port of entry but does not guarantee admission into the United States.

Further Reading

Annerino, John. *Dead in Their Tracks: Crossing America's Desert Borderlands.* New York: Four Walls Eight Windows, 1999.

Castañeda, Jorge G. *Ex Mex: From Migrants to Immigrants.* New York: The New Press, 2013.

Merino, Noel. *Illegal Immigration.* San Diego: Greenhaven Press, 2015.

Gonzales, Manuel. *Mexicanos: A History of Mexicans in the United States.* Bloomington and Indianapolis: Indiana University Press, 1999.

Hart, Elva Treviño. *Barefoot Heart: Stories of a Migrant Child.* Tempe, Ariz.: Bilingual Press/Editorial Bilingüe, 1999.

Martinez, Rubén. *Crossing Over: A Mexican Family on the Migrant Trail.* New York: Metropolitan Books, 2001.

Massey, Douglas S., Jorge Durand, and Nolan J. Maloone. *Beyond Smoke and Mirrors: Mexican Immigration in an Era of Economic Integration.* New York: Russell Sage Foundation, 2002.

Payan, Tony. *The Three U.S.-Mexico Border Wars: Drugs, Immigration, and Homeland Security.* Santa Barbara, Calif.: Praeger, 2016.

Thorpe, Helen. *Just Like Us: The True Story of Four Mexican Girls Coming of Age in America.* New York: Simon & Schuster, 2009.

Vallejo, Jody Agius. *Barrios to Burbs: The Making of the Mexican American Middle Class.* Stanford, Calif.: Stanford University Press, 2012.

Internet Resources

http://www.latinousa.org

This site gives listings and descriptions of shows on Latino USA, the only "national, English-language radio program produced from a Latino perspective."

http://www.maldef.org

The home page of this nonprofit advocacy group covers news and events and provides educational and employment services to Mexican Americans.

http://www.lulac.org

LULAC is the oldest Hispanic organization in the United States. Its home page provides useful information on the organization's programs as well as a comprehensive list of links to other sites.

http://www.nationalmuseumofmexicanart.org

This museum, located in Chicago, is the largest Mexican and Latino arts institution in the United States. The site offers updates on the latest exhibitions.

http://www.nclr.org

The website of the National Council of La Raza presents news and commentary on Mexican American political and economic issues.

Index

Numbers in **bold italic** refer to captions.

Contributors

Senior consulting editor STUART ANDERSON is an adjunct scholar at the Cato Institute and executive director of the National Foundation for American Policy. From August 2001 to January 2003, he served as executive associate commissioner for Policy and Planning and Counselor to the Commissioner at the Immigration and Naturalization Service. He spent four and a half years on Capitol Hill on the Senate Immigration Subcommittee, first for Senator Spencer Abraham and then as Staff Director of the subcommittee for Senator Sam Brownback. Prior to that, Stuart was Director of Trade and Immigration Studies at the Cato Institute, where he produced reports on the military contributions of immigrants and the role of immigrants in high technology. Stuart has published articles in the Wall Street Journal, New York Times, Los Angeles Times, and other publications. He has an M.A. from Georgetown University and a B.A. in Political Science from Drew University. His articles have appeared in such publications as the *Wall Street Journal*, *New York Times*, and *Los Angeles Times*.

MARIAN L. SMITH served as the senior historian of the U.S. Immigration and Naturalization Service (INS) from 1988 to 2003, and is currently the immigration and naturalization historian within the Department of Homeland Security in Washington, D.C. She studies, publishes, and speaks on the history of the immigration agency and is active in the management of official 20th-century immigration records.

PETER HAMMERSCHMIDT is director general of national cyber security at Public Safety Canada. He previously served as First Secretary (Financial and Military Affairs) for the Permanent Mission of Canada to the United Nations. Before taking this position, he was a ministerial speechwriter and policy specialist for the Department of National Defence in Ottawa. Prior to joining the public service, he served as the Publications Director for the Canadian Institute of Strategic Studies in Toronto. He has a B.A. (Honours) in Political Studies from Queen's University, and an MScEcon in Strategic Studies from the University of Wales, Aberystwyth.

JOSÉ RUIZ is a freelance writer and editor living outside Philadelphia, Pennsylvania. He has written several biographies for young adult readers.

Picture Credits